Tattered
and
Mended

TATTERED AND MENDED

THE ART *of* HEALING *the* WOUNDED SOUL

CYNTHIA RUCHTI

ABINGDON PRESS
NASHVILLE

Library of Congress Cataloging-in-Publication Data

Tattered and mended: the art of healing the wounded soul / Cynthia Ruchti.
  pages cm.
  Includes bibliographical references.
  ISBN 978-1-4267-8769-0 (binding: soft back)   1. Healing—Religious aspects—Christianity.   2. Spiritual healing.   I. Title.
  BT732.R83 2015
  242'.4—dc23

2015004748

Dedicated to those who bravely share
their tattered-soul stories
to give hope to those
in need of mending.

And to The Artistic Mender.

People are tattered.
Some say, "Then let's make tattered fashionable."
But God invites us to mend.

CONTENTS

INTRODUCTION

I'M NOT THE WRITER WHOSE PRIMARY AUDIENCE is theologians. I'm a writer who speaks to the single parent, the brokenhearted grandmother, the person reeling from a prickly divorce, the young woman who feels as awkward in the world as a harmonica in the orchestra, the working woman who doesn't usually have time to read nonfiction but will make time when she is handed a book by a trusted friend.

I write for the caregiver and the young widow and the older widow and the man or woman working three part-time jobs rather than one that could pay all the bills. I write for the jobless, the temporarily homeless, the speechless and dreamless and hopeless. The reader I hold to my heart as I write is the person who attends church regularly but isn't sure why, or the person for whom faith is as involuntary as breathing, and for the person who almost closed the covers of the book because of the word *faith*.

Most of us walk through weeks or seasons or lifetimes when we ask "Why me?" as life's circumstances shred our souls. I've heard the stories or lived them. If you extract strength or courage from these pages, it will be because your story intersects with God's story. I am an *observer*-writer. I see and watch and feel and then attempt to express what others struggle to put into words.

With my favorite lamp illuminating the desk, my favorite mug near it, and my fingers resting on the worn keys of my computer a little more than a year ago, I wrote a three-line premise that seemed to come not from my mind, but the deep end of my soul. It lingered with me, like a neglected but beloved pet begging for attention.

People are tattered.

Some say, "Then let's make tattered fashionable."

But God invites us to mend.

Tattered is not an irreversible condition, a label that indelibly marks us, our lot in life, or just-the-way-things-are-good-luck-with-that. Yes, what happens to us at the hands of others or as a result of our own poor judgment and mistakes can leave us battered and frayed on a soul level. God invites us to mend under his artistic hand and eye.

Brittle photographs damaged by sun exposure, creasing, or soot. Centuries-old artwork. Millenia-old pottery. Shredded jeans and moth-eaten sweaters and tattered quilts and the frayed edges of a historically significant tapestry. Once-vital health. A promising relationship. The job you thought perfect for you. The friendship you hoped would never fade. Your battered soul.

Beyond hope?

People are tattered—either more so these days than people once were, or more *obviously* so. Communication advances mean we hear about them almost as they're happening. A popular approach is to adapt then to tatteredness and resign ourselves to the hopelessness of it all, which not only keeps us broken but convinces us healing is impossible... or worse, unnecessary.

Onto that scene comes the Divine Invitation—God calling us to himself to find healing for our raked-raw souls. The invitation is to watch the progress of his intricate, meticulous, compassion-rich artistry. It's an invitation to lose our fears of the process and engage with him for our mending.

This is a book without formulas. It's a book of observation—

finding hope in ancient and modern mending techniques, stories of people with concerns like yours, and a gallery of wounds that have become works of art.

In some circles, tattered has become so fashionable that we can't tell the homeless from the tasteless. That's not a denegration of the homeless or a commentary on fashion trends, but an invitation to consider how that might translate to our internal health, our soul's health. Have we become comfortable with our tatteredness, our brokenness? Rather than resign ourselves to desperately cling to fragile shreds of recovery, rather than discard our broken, threadbare, scarred relationships, we can rediscover the art of mending.

I'll meet you in the pages.

—Cynthia

CHAPTER ONE

THE ART OF MENDING THE SOUL

People are tattered. Some say,
"Then let's make tattered fashionable."
But God invites us to mend.

HE WOKE THAT BLEACHED-OUT MORNING WITH the taste of dust in his mouth. Sleeping on the ground will do that to a person. He pushed himself to a sitting position and only rubbed the sleep from his eyes because the crusty bits hurt, not because they interfered with his line of sight.

The sound of movement beside him pressed him to reach for the water bottle he'd used as a pillow in the night. It was gone. He tapped the ground in an arc far wider than the distance where it had lain. Some street kid thought it was funny to swipe the homeless guy's water supply. Nice.

The man drew the ragged edges of his coat tight around him, a ridiculously inadequate protection. But it was all he had. The sun on his face felt warmest at chin-level. Not much past dawn. He stood, the ache in his bones more familiar and pronounced every day.

With his hand pressed against the stone wall that had been at his back through the night, he felt his way to the corner and waited, ears attentive. He crossed the cobbled street, arms extended, head bent. Another stone wall greeted his outstretched hands. He followed it to its end, the stubbled grasses now underfoot.

If he kept one sandal on dirt and the other on stubble, he could walk a straight line to the spot where the air on his face cooled slightly. Under the shade of the olive tree, he'd spend his day wrestling with himself. If a beggar didn't look pathetic, who would notice him? If he did, how could he retain any thread of dignity?

He could have made something of his life . . . if he weren't blind.

That may not be how morning started for Bartimaeus, as the gospel story recounts. But it might not be far from the truth. We have so many unanswered questions from his story told by Mark in the Bible.

Jesus and his followers came into Jericho. As Jesus was leaving Jericho, together with his disciples and a sizable crowd, a blind beggar named Bartimaeus, Timaeus' son, was sitting beside the road. When he heard that Jesus of Nazareth was there, he began to shout, "Jesus, Son of David, show me mercy!" Many scolded him, telling him to be quiet, but he shouted even louder, "Son of David, show me mercy!"

Jesus stopped and said, "Call him forward."

They called the blind man, "Be encouraged! Get up! He's calling you."

Throwing his coat to the side, he jumped up and came to Jesus.

Jesus asked him, "What do you want me to do for you?"

The blind man said, "Teacher, I want to see."

Jesus said, "Go, your faith has healed you." At once he was able to see, and he began to follow Jesus on the way. (Mark 10:46-52)

So many unanswered questions.

What was daily life like for Bartimaeus before that moment? Did he eat dust for breakfast? Where were his friends? What besides his coat did he leave behind when he followed Jesus? What future might he have had once he regained his sight? And how would that have looked if he'd decided to remain a beggar after he could see?

The crowd treated him as if he were a disturbance, when he was actually the object of God's attention.

Tucked between the folds of those seven short verses are insights your heart may be waiting for. Mine was.

The scene takes place in Jericho, an historically rich setting—a place where God did the impossible in a hopeless situation through unusual means. You can read about Jericho's history in Joshua 6. In Bartimaeus's time, the setting itself spoke of possibilities and hope.

Bartimaeus had no livelihood, other than begging. Losing his sight—if he ever had any—stripped his soul. His blindness prevented him from participating in the norms of society, including work.

He sat at the side of the road, choking on the dust of the passersby. Then his ears picked up on activity uncommon to their area. A celebrity and his entourage walked right in front of Bartimaeus.

Desperate enough to believe Jesus might have an answer when no doctor had, Bartimaeus shouted, "Jesus, Son of David, show me mercy!"

The crowd tried to silence the unruly beggar. "Quiet down. You're making a scene!" He shouted all the louder. "Son of David, show me mercy!"

The cry of a tattered soul.

Jesus instructed his entourage to call the man forward.

The disciples told the beggar, "Be encouraged! Get up! He's calling you."

So many times the disciples misunderstood who Jesus was, what he came to do, why he would care about the homeless and destitute and desperate, the broken, the tattered, the shattered. This time, it seems, they got it. They encouraged Bartimaeus, comforted him, even before anything further happened. It was honor enough that Jesus had called for him.

The beggar did something surprising in response. He not only rose to his feet, he jumped up. And he threw his coat aside to get to Jesus without encumbrance. What homeless person doesn't cling fiercely, protectively, to his coat and anything the pockets hold, naturally obsessed with those scraps of possessions?

Jesus didn't start his interaction with the soul-wounded

beggar by listing the man's failings or pronouncing him instantly cured or warning him that he'd better get his act together. Jesus asked, "What do you want me to do for you?" He extended an invitation.

The world's most rhetorical question?

From other passages of Scripture, we learn that Jesus knew people's needs, their minds, and their hearts without being told. Why *that* question?

Bartimaeus would have gone to his grave a blind man if he hadn't responded. I wonder how many milliseconds ticked off before the blind man said, "Teacher, I want to see." Did he pause a moment to consider what might have lain behind that "What can I do for you?" Was there something in the holy hush of that scene—a place where God made *impossible* things happen in *hopeless* situations through *unusual* means—that convinced Bartimaeus it was a question far deeper and more life-altering than it appeared on the surface?

He'd shouted his desperate plea for mercy. Now he had the ear of the Mercy-Giver. What did the beggar most need? His eyesight restored? Or something more?

His ache reached soul-deep. His need had a spiritual component as well as physical, societal, and emotional factors. "I want...I need...to see."

Jesus said, "Go, your faith has healed you."

But Bartimaeus didn't go, didn't pick up his tattered life where he'd left it along the side of the road. He could instantly see—on every level. The no-longer-a-beggar, no-longer-blind Bartimaeus trained his newly sighted eyes on the back of Jesus' cloak. The Bible tells us he "began to follow Jesus on the way."

He left all the possibilities now open to him for the honor of following Jesus. I wonder if one of the disciples ran back to grab the beggar's coat for him.

The tattered and wounded line roadways, courtrooms, breakrooms at work, family rooms, churches, hospital corridors. You may be one of them. How would you answer if Jesus asked, "What do you want me to do for you?"

Because Jesus *is* asking. It is the Divine Invitation to mend.

You might answer, "Stop these migraines!" or "What a ridiculous question. Can't you see I'm still reeling from the offenses against me in childhood?" or "PTSD. Ever heard of it?" or "I have three children with autism," or "My mother-in-law is out to destroy me," or "This recent job loss has completely drained me of all self-respect," or "I can't even define it, but of all people, I thought you'd know."

This is the detail I'd too long missed, a detail that changes everything. God doesn't just heal wounded souls. He heals us artfully.

God creates art from our brokenness. For Bartimaeus, the divine mend changed every aspect of his life, including what he did from that moment on, his gait, his perception of the world around him. He saw colors and shapes, saw the textures he'd only felt before, saw expressions on people's faces and pain in their eyes—a pain he would watch lift as people encountered Jesus as he had.

For centuries, the artistic have reclaimed exquisite beauty from the ragged, frayed, shattered, bent, damaged, disfigured, and unraveled—mending what was once thought beyond repair. The same can happen with the human soul.

God calls us to mend, to heal, to breathe into our aching lungs the invigorating air of wholeness, to experience the gratitude and sweet exhaustion of having come through, having found him an expert and artistic mender.

The medical facility in a town near my home boasts a dramatic new interior design. For years, a portion of the main lobby has been devoted to an art gallery. It could have been housed in a storefront downtown, or near the mall, or in a stand-alone building with an avant-garde architectural style that shouts, "ART!"

Instead, the gallery is tucked into a massive medical complex that sees thousands of patients every day, most of whom would rather be anywhere other than the clinic. They come in hobbled, wheelchair-bound, with casts and canes and light-obliterating sunglasses, with gauze-wrapped heads and neck braces and expressions that say, "I'm here for my biopsy" before the words spill from their mouths.

They come in pairs—the dad pushing his son in a wheelchair or vice versa. The mom and her twenty-ish daughter with four-year-old tendencies. The young couple pushing a stroller and an IV stand.

They come for diabetes checkups and depression help, for cataracts and chronic coughs, pain management and prenatal exams.

And many of them take a detour through the gallery. A detour from their mess to the quiet room with soft music, ambient lighting, and art. Someone in the clinic's history understood the healing power of art.

The gallery recently expanded to include mini displays of pottery, blown glass, and other works of master artists at the ends of elevator halls and in the windowed display cases that form one wall of the cafeteria. The cafeteria. Beef stroganoff and a little art. A discussion about the fresh diagnosis...and a little art.

From the simplest appointment to the most unnerving, I try to allow time for a visit to the gallery to take in the latest exhibit. I did so again today. Watercolors and stained glass panels filled the room. It doesn't escape notice that so much of what we call art is an artistic expression of the broken, the incomplete, the rejected, the pain-wracked yet inspiring.

An artist finds beauty in an abandoned farmhouse; a broken split-rail fence; the one handleless cup that doesn't match any of the others in the scene; weeds hugging the edges of a vacant lot; an empty walnut shell; an elderly, bent man on a park bench; the gnarled hand of a grandmother holding the flawless, dimpled hand of a newborn. A single spent rosebud lying at the base of a lush bouquet. A candle tucked inside a shattered-and-glued water pitcher, light streaming through all the crooked spaces. The exquisite teardrop clinging to the toddler's face. The exquisite toddler. The rusty door hinge, telling a thousand stories. The satin finish of the hand carved wood bowl, its fascinating design imprinted into the wood centuries ago by what then were considered destructive insects.

The artist sensed beauty there, and communicated it to us, the art appreciators.

Life is a gallery of scenes of beauty in the tattered.

Our Creator is not insensitive to the weariness of a soul

long tattered. He's more keenly aware than we are of the length and severity of each snag, the fragility of the thin spots, the acutely tender soul bruises. We feel them. He sees *and* feels them. He knows where they came from. He flinches with each new injury. He is, as the Bible tells us, "intimately familiar with suffering" (Isaiah 53:3 ISV).

This is the God who calls himself Healer. "I am the LORD who heals you" (Exodus 15:26). The Hebrew word for "Lord" in that verse is *Jehovah-Rophe,* or *Jehovah-Raphe/Rapha,* which doesn't merely name him "The God Who Can Heal" or "The God Who Heals" but "God *Your* Healer." A personal connection between us and The Mender.

This life-adjusting viewpoint of who God is at his core appeared first in Exodus 15. It referenced the children of Israel finally freed from slavery in Egypt, but facing starvation and dehydration with no source of water in the desert. They traveled for three days, searching for water and found none, until they came to Marah.

Imagine their relief. Their children and elderly—who suffered the most severely from the lack—would live. Their thirst could be quenched.

But no. The waters at Marah were undrinkable. Bitter. Unsafe.

Moses gave the people of Israel a new name for their

God—*Jehovah Rapha*, Your Healer—when God turned the bitter, unsafe water into sweet. Everyone's need, met.

Sweet, refreshing, whole.

Although God could and often did heal physical infirmities, this cherished, hope-giving name catapulted into the world as a result of the kind of mending we often most need—converting soul misery into something we can live with, wholeness where holes once dominated, raw edges sewn together expertly so they can't unravel again.

"I can't unravel. I'm hemmed in hope," the sticky note hanging on the edge of my computer screen reminds me.

Your Healer. My Healer. The one who specializes in mending the bitter so thoroughly it becomes sweet.

Medical science reports the mother's womb is such a healing-rich environment that babies operated on in utero often emerge at birth with no sign of a scar. No evidence of the surgery.

In that womb setting, that environment closest on earth to the perfection of Eden-before-human-intervention, God brings about a healing so complete there's no trace of a scar.

This side of the womb, scars show. Skillful surgeons can minimize their visibility, tuck them into natural creases in our skin, hide them under a hairline. But in the right light, scars can be artistic, revealing the imprint of The Healer.

When we're left tattered, scraped raw, frayed, ripped apart, tugging on the sleeves of our selves to cover deep emotional bruises, Jesus invites us—as he invited Bartimaeus—to come and mend. It is the core of his gospel, and the end product of his expertise.

We're not accustomed to mending. Darning eggs—a tool, not a food—are considered antiques. Did you have to Google "darning eggs" to make sense of that sentence, to know *darning* can be an adjective? That's how foreign it is to some of us when talking about socks with holes worn through. Who pulls the darning needle from the sewing basket—*who has a sewing basket?*—spreads the hole over a darning egg, and patches a sock anymore? When life rubs a sock raw, one of two things happens. The sock is tossed with little remorse into either the wastebasket or the rag bag. A hole makes it disposable.

And when marriages get frayed around the edges? When a friendship suffers a ripped seam? When disappointment slashes what look like bear claw tears in the fabric we thought could protect us? When faith wears through?

You can mend.

A whisper-sound. Firm, but gentle as a celestial sigh.

Mend. Staying tattered doesn't make you more real. It makes you ragged.

Historians tell us that ancient fabrics often reveal artistic touches—embroidered flowers, birds, appliques, large hand-carved buttons, other embellishments—which on careful observation are shown to cover what had once been a flaw in the fabric, a worn spot, a tear. Rather than coarsely stitching the rough edges together, a tailor or seamstress with an artistic eye transformed the garment into something even more elegant or intriguing than the original item.

That's the approach God takes. He can leave us in better shape—stronger, braver, more beautiful—than before we had a problem.

He isn't a halfway healer.

He never left a blind man partially sighted. Jesus didn't perform half-miracles. He didn't advocate that we could be "okay" but rather that we could be mended. Whole. No longer tattered.

Jesus mends.

"He heals the brokenhearted and *ignores* their wounds." No. The psalmist's lyrics were these: "He heals the broken-hearted / And binds up their wounds" (Psalm 147:3 NKJV).

He mends. He sutures. He slathers salve on the injured area and wraps it in holy bandages presoaked in mercy. Then, under his divine touch, wounds heal. Even wounds that cut bone-deep or leave raised-welt scars.

"He heals the brokenhearted and *makes headlines* from their wounds"?

"...and *celebrates* their wounds"?

"...and *creates museums* from their wounds"?

No. He mends.

It's no haphazard patch job, no Milwaukee Brewers sticker slapped over the boo-boo on a car's bumper. (Ask me where that analogy came from.) No spiritual duct tape or multiple crosshatched rubber bands. No grime-collecting Ace bandages.

His mending is artistry. Restoration is his specialty. Renewing broken things is his heart. Reclaiming shattered souls—repairing tattered lives—his preoccupation.

Everything he does is rooted in an invitation for us to "Come."

The Divine Invitation is to come-sit-heal and discover the art in God's artistic stitching.

This book is part of that invitation to think about soul-mending as a divine art form and about what it takes to experience healing on a soul-deep level. May you too find an artful relief for the tattered places in your soul as you walk through a gallery of the reclaimed and restored, explore mending techniques now celebrated as art, reflect on a tapestry of stories of the tattered and mended, and discover a pattern of hope for your hurt.

CHAPTER TWO

SASHIKO AND BORO RESCUE

Elegance from the Tattered

If mending were easy, we'd all do it.
If it couldn't be beautiful, none of us would.

A DIZZYING VOLUME OF IMAGES FLASHED ON THE computer screen as I scrolled through files of ancient mending techniques. I stopped scrolling when I landed on a page with intricate, precise stitches that formed tight patterns—parallel lines, spirals, boxes, the shape of gingko leaves.

Two-hundred-year-old Japanese garments we would consider rags now hang on museum walls, celebrated for the precision needlework that gave both stability and artful sophistication to tattered indigo. Not only did the *sashiko* mending technique keep the garment from being discarded or used for banal, mess-mopping purposes, the mends formed aesthetically intriguing patterns and textures. The mending elevated the pieces from common to artistic, from shredded to strong, from shelved to honored.

Imagination leads me to a humble villager's hut centuries ago. Smoke from the cooking fire dances with the smell of garlic and seared meat. In a corner near the window, where light and a table passed from generation to generation forms a work station, a woman chooses a piece of indigo to lay over a worn spot on a garment patched many times. She threads the stiff needle and holds it, pausing to consider the piece before her.

Had she sketched a pattern in her mind the night before? Did previous patches dictate where her new stitches should fall?

I can almost feel the pressure she feels when the needle pierces the fabric. By the time she works the needle in and out four or five times, a pattern has been established. In the simplicity and in some ways deprivation of her life, she refuses to make the patch ordinary.

Can you envision the expression on her face when what emerges from her humble mending is art? Can you picture what her expression would look like if she could have known the garment she repaired would one day be considered museum-quality? And how could she know that the process in which she engaged expressed the heart of a mending God?

Under his care, the human soul can be elevated from a state of incessant pain to a place of healing that not only strengthens the shredded but also reveals a new depth of refinement created during the mending process—from the stitches themselves.

The tiny, exacting stitches of sashiko reinforce weak places, worn corners, or form solid connections for life-extending patches. Traditionally, homespun fabrics woven from tree-bark fibers, hemp, wisteria, or grasses were dyed with indigo, plentiful and easily accessible. Sashiko stitching in the early traditions like the scene in my imagination were pale cotton thread—white—a dramatic contrast against the deep blue. Extra care was taken to stitch precisely, in a measured way with evenly spaced threads, in the long running stitch that created a series of simple designs that have become a highly prized art form today.

In our frayed state—betrayed, rejected, neglected, bullied,

pathologically disappointed, attacked, or exhausted by an endless pounding of crises, divinely designed reinforcing stitches—anchoring stitches—hem us in hope. They can form an intentional pattern of mending that generations to come admire.

Can what I'm going through mean something to someone else? The pattern grief etches across the surface of my soul isn't random and purposeless? No, it isn't. Even if it takes a thousand needle pinpricks on the fabric of my soul, a pattern can emerge against the dark backdrop. A pattern that spells healing. Hope.

Hope stitched in delicate rows on a background I thought devoid of promise.

I'm filling a Pinterest board with examples of sashiko and other decorative mending techniques. It's a board I'll turn to when life gets uncomfortable, or when my thoughts return to times I—like many—wonder what God is doing.

"Oh. He's making art."

Shortly after writing that last sentence, my husband's job disintegrated like a snowflake on hot asphalt. The second time in recent years. A company buy-out forced the first. Downsizing, the second. This last time felt like a switchblade slicing through flesh. A year from retirement. Too close to unemployable. Too far from Medicare or other help.

The call came when I was out of town serving at a conference. In the hours and days after the call, reality widened the wound. We'd been frugal, careful. But frugal wouldn't be enough to fill the gap. And frugal wouldn't mend my husband's wounded ego.

Almost instantly, the crisis proved it would also test our marriage in new—though not altogether unfamiliar—ways. Financial concerns remain among the top stressors for many marriage relationships. We hadn't escaped them. Despite our commitment to each other over the course of more than four decades together, we still have to work hard to keep discussions about money worries and expenditures from damaging the fabric of our marriage. I knew my husband had been crushed by the announcement that his position had been eliminated. Again. And I bore my own wounds. The kind of uncertainty this news brought could have been indicted for disturbing the peace.

Would I be able to continue to follow my passion to write and speak? Would my husband's unemployment force me into other work that paid better but didn't hold my heart? Would we need to return to the days of monotonous meals of ring bologna and rice, our early marriage staples?

Both the loss of income and the perceived loss of meaning

in his work history threatened to create a soul tatter, to figuratively tear my husband's career into rags.

We're still in the process of watching God stitch sashiko-style reinforcement over this ragged spot. The stitches look something like this:

- God is faithful. He is faithful. He is faithful.

- God is not unaware of our need.

- God's provided in the past. He will again.

- God knew this was coming before we did. He has answers prepared already.

- God won't abandon us in trying times. He draws nearer. Nearer. Nearer.

I could hear in my husband's voice the deep sorrow that had settled over him when he called to tell me what had happened. My instinct was to offer encouraging words and somehow bequeath him my confidence that we were going to be okay, as if offering him a bite of my steak when he'd ordered fish sticks. I held back, sensing that what he most needed at that moment wasn't clear to me yet.

It's no surprise I found direction in the pages of God's word, and more solid stitching for my own frayed edges.

The prophet Jeremiah lamented over the cruelty thrust on God's people, the way their enemies clawed them. In Jeremiah 8:11, the prophet said, "They treat the wound of my people / as if it were nothing: / 'All is well, all is well,' they insist, / when in fact nothing is well."

Across the page in verse 21 of that chapter my eyes fell on these compassionate words: "Because my people are crushed, / I am crushed."

And capping the perspective-shaper, chapter 9 offered startling insight for me, in that mending holding cell where I waited. "Women, hear the LORD's word. Listen closely to the word / from his mouth: / teach your daughters to mourn; / teach each other to grieve" (Jeremiah 9:20).

My instinct was to comfort. God was asking me to grieve better? To mature in mourning? Dark stitches among the light?

An ancient proverb says that "Singing a song to a troubled heart / is like taking off a garment on a cold day / or putting vinegar on a wound" (Proverbs 25:20).

My role, initially, included accepting responsibility to feel my husband's grief, to be crushed because he was, but then to hold the task light over the fabric so the stitching could begin.

For my soul's wounds and his, mending started with God's words. Truths that applied to Jeremiah's concerns and ours, to ancient times and the twenty-first century, to enemy armies and empty bank accounts, to the book of Job and the book of job loss.

"Heal me, LORD, and I'll be healed. / Save me and I'll be saved, / for you are my heart's desire" (Jeremiah 17:14). A confession from the same Jeremiah whose soul was crushed with concern over his people. His lament wasn't complete without his declarations of faith.

I wouldn't have seen the connecting threads if I hadn't sought the essential anchoring knots of truth in the Truth Text—the Bible. How long would centuries-old sashiko stitches have lasted if there'd been no knot at the end of the thread?

Whatever the crisis, it all unravels if I forget to anchor my thoughts in what God's word says.

Those fighting an endless battle to stay afloat financially might answer, "God is my Provider. But it doesn't look like he's—"

God is my Provider. End of statement.

> "My God will meet your every need out of his riches in the glory that is found in Christ Jesus" (Philippians 4:19).

24

Those facing legal battles would think long and hard, then answer, "He is my Defender."

"God, my strength, I am looking to you, / because God is my defender" (Psalm 59:9 NCV).

Those churning with anxiety: "He is my Peace."

"Christ is our peace" (Ephesians 2:14).

Those sliced open by abandonment or neglect issues: "He is Ever-present."

"God is our refuge and strength, / a help always near in times of great trouble" (Psalm 46:1).

Those still battered by past abuse: "He is my Healer."

"I am the LORD who heals you" (Exodus 15:26).

The atmosphere at a recent open-air worship service seemed charged with an electricity that humbled the lightning that threatened from the horizon's storm. It was a before-and-after service, an opportunity for people once ragged and tattered to tell their stories of how they were mended or mending.

I noticed several common threads as the stories unfolded.

- A prior sense of aloneness until those telling their stories recognized God had been there all along.

- A once strongly held belief that their circumstances were hopeless, until God and his people convinced them differently.

- A radical shift in their thinking. They consciously distanced themselves from their past and its hurts.

- Gratitude that made them braver than their natures and often spilled over into tears.

In the audience were those with a story they weren't yet willing to tell. They had one—the tattered story they'd lived with too long, the rag of a story they'd clung to like a child who refuses to let go of a threadbare, grimy blanket.

The people who were healed by Jesus began with one step. They came to him or were presented to him by friends. They didn't run away. They followed his sometimes extremely detailed directions about the investment he wanted them to make, like the kinds of investments of time, effort, and desire required for our healing.

Everything they did—the people Jesus healed in the Bible—was an act of, maybe a test of, obedience and faith. *Wash seven times. Let me put mud on your eyes. Rise and walk. Take up your mat.* They didn't make themselves well. The effort they exerted related to their surrender to the process. Many of them were too broken, too shattered to do more than sigh.

To no one did Jesus say, "Recite these five random words forty times and you'll be healed." Or, "Swing a chicken over your head and bark like a dog." Or "Let me see you in synagogue for the next twelve Sabbaths in a row, and if you memorize the book of Deuteronomy, your healing will appear before the next full moon."

We won't know that for sure, won't know how he mends, unless we know what God's word does say. Opening those pages is threading the needle for the healing to begin.

– – – – –

Jerome's hands shook violently, spilling coffee on his open Bible. One pronounced slosh. It created a cloudlike stain on the page. What were the odds the slosh would have landed on the one verse to which he'd clung since he entered prison, the verse he ran to like he once ran to drugs—hungrily, desperately? Especially on the days—and nights—when he feared for his life. Which was every day. Every night.

The murderer against whom Jerome had been asked to testify showed up in the same prison unit. That wasn't supposed to happen. It soon became evident that the inmate who had often joined Jerome in the courtyard to play guitar—"Music hath charms"—was the murderer's close friend. Jerome watched them from across the prison yard as they talked under their breath and cast searing glances his way.

No television drama. Real life. Real Midwestern life.

Fear sliced through Jerome's soul. He knew the kinds of crimes that happen behind bars—as intense and violent as anything on the other side of the razor wire.

He'd dropped his past way of thinking, his unwise and illegal decisions, shortly after his incarceration began. Hints of the God he'd heard about on the outside pierced through the cement walls into his cell. It shocked him to consider that God's lavish love was meant for him, even him. When he embraced it, grateful that what Jesus paid for with his life included Jerome's sins, too, he changed from darkness to light...on the inside.

But he had a societal debt to pay, which kept him locked in an external darkness. Lurking in the darkness now was a murderer bent on revenge.

Jerome's eyes landed on the coffee stained verse as he sat in his cell, more doubtful than ever that he'd *walk* out of prison when his sentence was complete rather than be carried out prematurely. Through the stain, he read, "I know the plans I have in mind for you, declares the LORD; they are plans for peace, not disaster, to give you a future filled with hope" (Jeremiah 29:11).

A cloud of fear, with God's love spreading its "stain" over all.

His wife told me, "I've seen that page of his Bible. It's beautiful."

Art.

"A future filled with hope."

Two weeks shy of his release date, a new inmate—the stereotypical bouncer/bodyguard/hitman whom Jerome had seen conversing with the murderer and his cohorts—approached Jerome and handed him a manila envelope. He said he'd been instructed by the murderer to "take care of this issue." Jerome didn't have to wonder what that meant—prison language for a permanent "accident."

The envelope held the transcript of Jerome's conversation with the detectives when he'd been asked to testify. The new inmate had been enlisted to carry out the deed. Instead, by what we can only assume was God's grace—part of a "future filled with hope" for Jerome—the inmate handed him the damning testimony and said, "Hey, man. I think you should have this. I understand why you did what you did," and walked away.

The next day, the murderer's close friend was transferred to a prison in another state. Two weeks later, Jerome was released.

He walked out into freedom. Filled with hope.

The verse that accompanied him through his when-it-all-falls-apart fears now forms portions of the intricate stitching of his reclaimed life.

— — — — —

The history of another Japanese mending practice—*boro*—shows the contrast between our habit of discarding the worn and the ancient practice of preserving or revitalizing the worn.

The term *boro* literally translates as scraps or rags of cloth, patched and repaired many times, perhaps even longer than the lifetime of its owner. Family sagas live between the stitches.

A *bodoko*, or "life-cloth" constructed from layers of worn pieces of cloth patched many times, served as a bed sheet in daily family life. At the birth of a baby, the bodoko was hung by ropes from the ceiling and stretched across the floor for the birthing woman to kneel on. The first thing the newborn touched was the many-layered, many-storied bodoko, the embrace of ancestral history and a connection to the family from which and into which it was born.

Boro coats—rags made beautiful—hang behind protective glass in prestigious art museums today, beside the intricate sashiko, a testament to endurance and to time invested to waste nothing and use everything.

We have access to the fiber art pieces—sashiko, boro—because of careful attention of ordinary people long ago who wove beauty into practicality, who never lost sight of the value of the simple or the worth of mending torn places so the garment—or the marriage, the friendship, the relationship—could last a lifetime. Or more.

Mending techniques like sashiko and boro require needles. *Sashiko* literally means "little stabs." The mending process isn't always a comfortable one. But it's necessary to keep us from falling apart.

Among my earliest crystal-clear memories of childhood are the years' worth of monthly penicillin shots my mother—a nurse—administered to my backside because of a bout of rheumatic fever when I was two. It was the accepted wisdom of the day. I fought those injections like any good toddler would. Even today, I remember the tension that commandeered my body when my mother would prepare the metal—

yes, metal—syringe and six-foot-long needle. That's an estimate from my toddler memories.

Every cell in me tensed and rebelled against the moment. I'd lie on my stomach, squirming so badly I defined the concept of *moving target.* My mother—tougher than my Marine father—always won the battle. I must have exhausted her with my resistance to a pinprick that lasted a few seconds at most and was designed to protect my weakened immune system.

Mom knew better than to ask, "Are you ready?" I would never have been ready.

"I'll never be ready to forgive my stepfather for the way he ruined my childhood," a tattered soul might say. "And if forgiveness is part of mending my soul, then I guess there's no hope for mending."

Can you and I trust God to deal adequately with those who have wronged us? Are we afraid he'll either let them get away with the heinous things they've done, or worse—he'll show them mercy?

Isn't that at the heart of our resistance? What if God decides to love them rather than punish them for what they've done? We're okay with the idea that he'll rain misery on their lives or condemn them to a suffering far more intense—if possible—

than our own. Are we okay with it if he shows them extravagant love and redeems their miserable lives? Is that what we're
afraid of when we cling to resentment and unforgiveness?

"Somebody has to hold them accountable for what they've
done. If not me—their victim—than who? I want to believe
God will. But he tosses mercy around like free candy at a
parade."

We wouldn't voice those thoughts. Not even to ourselves.
But how far are they from the truth about what our feelings
tell us?

"Forgiveness doesn't excuse (other people's) behavior. Forgiveness prevents their behavior from destroying your heart,"
wrote Trisha Davis. She learned the width and breadth of forgiveness following her husband's infidelity. Now, in a display
of artistry only God could orchestrate, Trisha and Justin help
other troubled couples find healing.

Forgiveness—which ushers in a wave of healing balm for a
tattered soul—is rooted in our trusting God to handle an injustice, clinging to the belief that however he chooses to manage
it is right, because he's always right. Rightness or righteousness
and justness or justice are inescapable, unshakable tenets of
his character. "I am the LORD who acts with kindness, / justice,
and righteousness in the world, / and I delight in these things, /

declares the LORD," reads Jeremiah 9:24. He doesn't have to be convinced to do the right thing. He delights in justice.

The wounded soul isn't always present at the confrontation between the one who inflicted the injury and the God of justice. Surrendering our front-row seats for that event is part of our healing process.

– – – – –

The first evening's session of a weekend-long retreat in the Northwoods began traditionally—an introduction, a little humor to connect with the crowd, and then a brief story coupled with a "take this back to your cabins" thought to ponder until the main sessions began the following morning.

A few minutes into what I'd prepared to share—the true story of my husband's Canadian adventure that almost took his life—a woman sitting halfway back on the left side of the chapel began to weep uncontrollably. Several friends moved to sit near her, where they stayed until I finished my part of the program. I'd offended her somehow, or inadvertently stabbed at some soul wound. I couldn't ignore her pain.

When the women dismissed to the dining hall for evening snacks and games, I excused myself and went immediately to the weeping woman in the chapel. I sat in the row in front of her, faced her, and said, "Please tell me how I've offended you."

Her friend answered for her. "You got your husband back. Hers died a month ago."

Hers had been to the doctor the day before and had committed to finally doing something about his diabetes. He'd eat better, he promised, starting right away the next morning. He'd exercise. He'd follow the protocol the doctor had long ago prescribed.

The mid-summer day dawned bright and alive with promise. Before he could implement any of his new commitments, his heart failed him and he was gone.

Devastated, lost, alone, crushed by the weight of what could have been, this mother of two stumbled through the funeral and the first weeks of a future completely unlike the one she'd envisioned. The love of her life had been extracted from the picture.

As this woman's story poured out, I gave her the only gift I had—a listening heart.

We've stayed in touch since that weekend. I've watched the sometimes excruciatingly slow process of mending for her ragged soul. Neither of us assumes the day will come when it no longer hurts that her husband died too soon. That would insinuate their marriage—and his life—didn't matter. But they did and they do. His absence left a canyon hole in their family. And canyon-sized patches are unwieldy.

But she's functioning better. Not because time heals. It doesn't have that much clout. She's functioning better because what was once excruciating is now tender. What was an open wound, frighteningly traumatized by the slightest breeze or speck of dust, now has a protective skin over it that leaves it less vulnerable. Her life will never be the same. But she knows now it can be good, despite the empty spot her husband once occupied.

She's grieving in her own way, milking every memory. But the grief is not a single-minded occupation or preoccupation anymore. It's a part of life, not the definition of it. And that's what reveals she's mending from the trauma, without dismissing the loss as meaningless.

I can do anything one time. Today, I'm going to trust. Or, this hour, this one hour, I'm going to trust. The Trusting Hour.

It's counterproductive for us to wait until we're ready to heal. We'll never be ready for the mending process. God invites us to heal anyway.

CHAPTER THREE

QUILT RECONSTRUCTION

An Artful Mend

*A quilt lovingly and carefully repaired
adds another chapter to its story.*

A YOUNG WOMAN REACHES INTO THE MUSTY trunk in her great-grandmother's attic and lifts out an ivory silk wedding gown. The fabric makes an appreciative rustling sound as it sees the light for the first time in many decades. Yards of fabric billow out of the trunk. What a treasure!

The young woman turns the gown to the back where hundreds of silk-covered buttons trace the path of an earlier bride's spine. She notes the waistline is narrow but should fit, if she sticks to her personal trainer's suggestions between now and her wedding day.

Holding the gown in her arms as tenderly as she would a sleeping or injured child, she carries it closer to the window, where she can inspect it further. Any stains? Torn lace? No. But as she fans the skirts, her heart plummets. Fine tears slice through the fabric, as if a razor ripped vertical lines at random intervals. The silk has shattered, disintegrated. And there's no mending shattered silk.

Vintage clothing experts tell us *shattered* is a term used to describe silk fibers that have split or deteriorated. The silk can be weakened from being weighted, hung, or stressed, or by the chemical effects of salt dying.

Silk was historically sold by weight: the heavier the fabric, the higher price it commanded. Some manufacturers processed silk with metallic salts which artificially increased the fabric's weight and the manufacturer's profits. The salts contained traces of tin or iron, which helped create the distinctive rustling noise which customers considered appealing and a sign of a quality product.

In time, the advantages were outweighed by the damage the salts created in the fabric—small tears that became big tears, as if the fabric were sliced with a razor blade.

The bride-to-be abandons her hopes of wearing the gown for her wedding. She searches the fabric for an intact scrap large enough to incorporate into the pattern of her memory's quilt.

– – – – –

I lay listening to—and feeling—the patternless pattern. A heartbeat is supposed to be a predictable set of sounds hovering in the background of life. Unnoticeable unless intentionally sought. A *tha-thump, tha-thump* that starts in the womb and continues unbroken until the end of life. Its pace increases or slows with exercise, sleep, an adrenaline rush, soft music, fear, infatuation, or the brush of a caring hand.

Tha-thump, tha-thump.

Not tha-thump…tha…tha-tha-tha thump…tha-thump. It's a hard tune to dance to.

That's the rhythm my heart started producing in the summer of 1984. The palpitations and irregular heartbeats shook my chest with their violence. Every cardiac test said my heart was rhythmically fickle but fine.

The next month, a new symptom joined the palpitations. Joint and muscle pain that migrated to different parts of my body as if on a poorly planned world tour jumped from one location to another with no logic or connection to how much or little I exercised.

Then the headaches crash-landed. Blinding, flattening headaches that lingered not just hours or days, but months. During the worst of it, the unwanted guest headache refused to leave for five months straight without even ten minutes' break. My doctor performed more tests, probed more possibilities, prescribed more medicinal options, most of which made the symptoms worse if they affected them at all.

The list of symptoms grew. I'd accidentally enrolled in the Discomfort-of-the-Month Club and couldn't find the Unsubscribe button. So many, so complicated, and so erratically bizarre. I created a spreadsheet to chart them for each medical specialist who wanted to know the whole story.

Muscle spasms. Vision problems. Facial numbness. Paralyzing fatigue.

I could read the message in my husband's eyes. He thought I might not survive whatever this was. I didn't disagree with him. My doctor offered nothing to reassure him.

Life swirled around me. Doctors' appointments and survival clogged the schedule. A new battery of tests. A new panel of medications.

Pain sent me to the couch. Determination pulled me off of

it to care for my two young children. Some scenes from those endless months, which turned into a year, which turned into a year and a half, remain vivid in memory. A neurologist—the eighth specialist I'd seen, the eighth with no answers and no relief to offer—suggested my symptoms were related to stress. Tests had eliminated every disease, malady, and disorder the medical community thought plausible. Stress. That had to be it.

His questions goaded.

The only true stress in my life lay embedded in the frustration of not knowing what was going on with my body. I'd started the journey sane, but wondered if insanity, death, or answers would come first.

Except for even darker circles under my eyes than normal, nothing about the medical crisis showed on the outside. In some ways, that complicated daily life. The palpitations that stole my breath and the joint and muscle pain that traveled an indirect route through my body every moment of the day stayed locked inside. Friends and family couldn't see the way my vision distorted. Super-charged nerve endings bolted at the sound of a door slamming on the other side of the house or in another exam room down the hall at the clinic. I should be grateful the tests showed nothing wrong, one doctor said, and move on.

"I would move on if I could move, Doc."

The response, too, stayed inside.

I couldn't write it to him in a note. My fingers couldn't hold a pencil or pen without excruciating pain.

Many reading these words know where this story is leading. Yes, I had Lyme disease, far less common in our area in the mid-1980s than it is today. By the time my never-give-up primary care physician discovered the culprit—or rather thousands of spirochete culprits and their cousins—it had established a stronghold deep in my cells, like a Sequoia driven into the ground to the depth of its limbs' armpits. That deep.

The first round of high-powered antibiotics provided a good chuckle for the tenacious Lyme spirochetes. The second raised little more than a ho-hum. A ten-day hospital stay, months into treating what now had a name, blasted the disease with millions of units of sword-wielding medicine every four hours around the clock.

And still, the battle raged inside.

Some symptoms abated, or shrank back temporarily. Some faded and didn't return. When my hands could hold a pencil again, I began picking up the broken bits of who I'd been before Lyme disease threw me against a wall, began assessing what remained intact of the life I once knew.

Like a frayed quilt, the basic structure hadn't changed. But how worn and detached and pattern-distorting Lyme disease had left it.

When a quilt suffers sun damage or rough use, or its threads weaken and seams pull apart, quilt restorers know they're in for an intense mending session, for a series of tests, diagnoses, attempts and more attempts before the shelved quilt can be put back into use. Is it worth saving? How can it be repaired with the least intrusion into or disruption of its original pattern? What materials will end up distorting the artistry, pulling and tugging unnaturally?

Sometimes quilt restoration requires the counsel of more than one expert to develop a plan that maintains authenticity and prevents further deterioration.

There is wisdom, the Bible tells us, in many counselors (Proverbs 15:22).

When life feels like a faded, tattered quilt, the intense gaze of onlookers analyzing what's wrong and how best to fix the spiritual and emotional damage can mimic the discomfort of a cadre of physicians shuffling a patient and his or her medical chart among them. Each with an opinion. None with a consensus.

During the Lyme disease siege, the last thing I wanted was

to listen to friends' or family's indignant grumbling about the doctors caring for me. Mysteries are mysterious, by nature. Logic drove the physicians to a pattern of tests. The negative test results drove them to conclude nothing was wrong...or that an emotional component explained the ever-growing, ever more convoluted list of symptoms. I had no energy for anger at the medical community. No heart for it either.

And although I appreciated the many, many—no, seriously, *many*—homegrown diagnosticians:

- "It must be multiple sclerosis."

- "My aunt had a couple of those symptoms...right before she died."

- "You might be allergic to milk."

- "Have you tried acupuncture?"

and attempted most of the home remedies, to no avail, underneath the chaos of pain breathed an incomprehensible peace. It—the peace—kept drawing in air when my lungs resisted. It pulsed when my heart merely fluttered—a peace many found startling in light of the medical threat. It was a peace that sang when I couldn't even sigh.

Peace—a gift from the heart of a caring, aware, empathetic

God. Exquisite. Like silk threads embroidered over a supposedly irreparable hole in an antique quilt.

I had nothing else to cling to but trust in the One who made me, the One best equipped to know both what was wrong and how to fix it. Every ounce of strength or ingenuity or reasoning I counted on before that first symptom hit had been shredded by the disease. Emptied of everything, I rediscovered my Everything.

Psalm 73:28 put it into words for me. "But as for me, the nearness of God is my good; / I have made the LORD GOD my refuge, / that I may tell of all Your works" (NASB).

His nearness—which sometimes felt like a silent but breath-altering Presence or an imperceptible whisper of hope or an embrace the Bible describes in a verse that says, "and underneath are the everlasting arms"—formed both comfort and protection for me while my body fought off the insidious invaders that had tugged at the connecting seams and pulled out the quilt batting of my soul (Deuteronomy 33:27 KJV).

While my body and mind were engaged in finding a name for the ailment and then finding the medicinal portal to conquer it, my spirit healed. Before we had the name or the cure. It healed not because I didn't care anymore. Certainly not because I didn't hurt anymore. But because my More-Than-Enough was.

This is hard. So hard. But God is near. So near. The confession held me while I waited for the embroidery work that would turn my emptiness into art.

I couldn't afford to get caught up in rage and anger about how long it took for the healing to begin. Anger drowns out the sound of God's comforting voice. It tears wildly and scrapes the soul more raw than it already is.

I chose instead to remember he'd been faithful in the past and chose to assume he would be again.

In some cultures, meditation plays a much stronger role than it does for many of us. My meditation thoughts during that time when I desperately needed mending focused on what I knew to be true about God. Some days, that's the only coherent thought I could form. For meditation to be effective, I had to jettison the lies about him or about me that I seemed especially vulnerable to when my physical body was at its weakest.

Lie: He doesn't care about details.

Truth: Ah, but he does.

Lie: God doesn't even know my name, much less my pain.

Truth: He knows the number of hairs on my head and the distinct sound of my groans.

Lie: My healing is dependent on the volume of my faith.

Truth: My healing is dependent on the power of my God.

Lie: Some things are too difficult even for God.

Truth: Nothing is too difficult for him.

The rebuttals didn't originate with me. They weren't works of imagination I hoped were true. I discovered them within the pages of God's word. From his own heart.

My intentionally meditative thoughts drew me to rehearse the heart-art of Psalm 139:1-4.

> LORD, you have examined me.
>
> You know me.
>
> You know when I sit down and when I stand up.
>
> Even from far away, you comprehend my plans.
>
> You study my traveling and resting.
>
> You are thoroughly familiar with all my ways.
>
> There isn't a word on my tongue, LORD,
>
> that you don't already know completely.

Reining them back from where they wandered on another wave of pain, another headache, another unnerving tsunami of dizziness, my thoughts followed a well-worn path to now familiar comforts. "But the LORD's faithful love is from forever ago to forever from now for those who honor him"

(Psalm 103:17). "But your loyal love, LORD, extends to the skies; / your faithfulness reaches the clouds" (Psalm 36:5).

"I cry out to you because you answer me. / So tilt your ears toward me now— / listen to what I'm saying! / Manifest your faithful love in amazing ways / because you are the one / who saves those who take refuge in you" (Psalm 17:6-7).

"I called to him for help, / and my call reached his ears" (Psalm 18:6).

"Going through the motions doesn't please you, / a flawless performance is nothing to you. / I learned God-worship / when my pride was shattered. / Heart-shattered lives ready for love / don't for a moment escape God's notice" (Psalm 51:16-17 THE MESSAGE).

"LORD God, you created heaven and earth by your great power and outstretched arm; nothing is too hard for you!" (Jeremiah 32:17).

I could have meditated on how many beats my heart missed. Or a new region of bone-deep pain. Or the list of things-I-can-no-longer-do. Even now, years later, I can't find one redeeming reason for locking my gaze on those things. They couldn't affect a cure and could only weaken my resolve and resilience. So I stayed aware of what the medical community needed to know, but meditated on hope.

Hope lay embedded in God's character, not in what I felt or could see from my flattened perspective.

Not trusting God's sovereignty would have been as much of a threat to my soul mending as metallic salts are to raw silk. Leaning into his sovereignty-dovetailed-with-his-intense-love safeguarded the process while I waited. It encapsulated me in a protective, yet oxygenated chamber—an atmosphere that promotes healing. Like climate control for mending an antique quilt.

As I waited on God—which in essence meant plain old waiting, keeping my focus directed on God while I did—hooked barbs tried to snag the soul healing, to undo the progress. *What if this never goes away? What if I never feel any better than I do today? What if God decides I deserve this or it's important to my training as an empathizer and there's no end date to the apprenticeship? What if when God sees the thoughts I'm thinking now, he snaps up his healing and goes home?*

Our attempts to keep secrets from God—as if that were possible—or our fears of what he might do in his efforts to help us mend smack of a panicked child who isn't thinking clearly and runs in circles when injured rather than running to the embrace of a parent. Or of Adam and Eve who thought they could hide their brokenness from God. From God's perspective, their hiding from him must have stabbed at his already aching, betrayed heart. "This is how little you know me?" God might have asked. "That you think you could hide your distress or that I wouldn't notice?"

As God mended what had been broken in me—both in body and spirit—I began to see that he wasn't merely replacing faded material or restitching seams that had loosened. He was embroidering a design that would forever remind me of the story of what I'd been through...and how near he drew.

CHAPTER FOUR

METAL RECYCLING

From Dumpster to Gallery

*What it used to be matters less than
the stunning work of art it has become.*

THEY TORE THE ROOF OFF THE AIRPORT.

Piece, by piece, workmen dismantled the historic copper roof of Lambert-St. Louis International Airport. Ripping a metal roof from the place it's lived for sixty years is complicated. A skyful of aged, bent, twisted copper lived temporarily in Dumpsters until recycling centers and art communities could get their hands on it.

Yes, art communities. A few green patina tiles were slated for use by St. Louis area print studios for creating exclusive prints for an art and culture fundraising event. The weathered tiles became printmaking plates for the imagery. The studios that were recipients of the tiles chose to leave the weathering marks forever impressed into the copper and, by association, impressed into the artwork created from them.

The end product looked nothing like it did in its beginnings. It had been an artful architectural element until life weathered it past a state useful for those purposes. But that didn't spell the copper's end. It spelled its mend, its genesis or regenesis into other shapes, other uses, and yet another reason for onlookers to say, "Oh, how beautiful!"

I knelt at the feet of a young woman in regenesis when I stopped in the prayer room of a conference. She sat alone, hands clasped, forearms on her thighs, bent at the waist and neck with a weight of disbelief over what had happened to her. I'd intended to quietly rest my hand on her shoulder as I passed through the room to my next responsibility. But I'd come to the quiet to be refreshed with God's word and had minutes earlier had my heart ripped open by what I found there. How could I callously pass by?

"Women, hear the LORD's word. Listen closely to the word from his mouth: / teach your daughters to mourn; / teach each other to grieve" (Jeremiah 9:20).

Again, God? I needed to hear that again? Mourning is a learned art? Grieving, a teachable skill?

I needed lessons. One sat a few feet from me. Crumpled. Shattered. Her husband had left her and their preschool-aged daughter and pressed for a divorce she didn't want. Her dream house for three turned into a cheesy downtown apartment for two, an apartment neither she nor her daughter could imagine anyone choosing. The mom's once-vibrant expectations for marriage had followed her husband out the door on his way to someone else.

I'd heard bits of her story a month earlier. She'd voiced her frustration through an essay on shopping for a pillow.

Her little girl had perfected the art of *surly*. Now working full-time and juggling daycare, preschool, and her grief, Mom had energy for little other than exasperation.

Everything seemed broken. The marriage that snapped in two. The future she'd imagined—shattered. The financial stability she'd come to lean on—gone. The concept of home— sliced in half with broken-glass edges.

My friend fought to hold back tears in the simplest tasks— grocery shopping, making meals, picking out a pillow for the couch.

A pillow for the couch. That's all she wanted. Something

fresh that would distinguish the old furniture in a new apartment from the life she thought she'd be living.

The meltdown that had been brewing within her for days happened in the pillow aisle of the home décor store. Couldn't even find a pillow. That's all she wanted. Just a pillow. A symbol of a new start. A sign that life could be okay again.

Nothing was right. The vast stock of pillows offered her the wrong shade of blue, the wrong texture, the wrong size. Nothing would ever be right again. Ever. It would never stop hurting.

As the tears fell, she could almost hear silk shattering in her soul.

Then, another sound. "Mommy? Mommy!"

Her petulant daughter had wandered out of sight. The fear in the young girl's voice changed the mother's perspective in an instant. She called out to her daughter, but the girl couldn't hear the calls over her own panicked cries. Finally the mother screamed her daughter's name—right there in the middle of the pillow aisle—and the lost was found.

Hopelessness drove the little girl's panic. She'd never find her mom in that huge store. Or maybe Mom had left her. Maybe she deserved it.

My friend assured her daughter she would never leave her

alone. It wasn't hopeless. She'd seen the flash of her daughter's blonde hair as the girl raced past the ends of the aisles, frantic for the mom who was standing right where she'd left her.

"What did I milk from that scene?" the young mom asked. "God sees me when I'm hopeless. Sees my panic and anxiety and fears. He sees my attitude and frustration and loves me anyway."

She rehearsed cherished verses. "The LORD is waiting to be merciful to you, / and will rise up to show you compassion" (Isaiah 30:18).

In Zechariah 1:14, God assured her and us, "I care passionately."

In Luke 1:67-79, we read these action words that the prophet Zechariah used to reveal God's true heart in our times of distress. "He has *come* to *help* and has *delivered* his people. / He has *raised up* a mighty savior for us. / ... He has *brought salvation* from our enemies / and from the power of those who hate us. / He has *shown* the *mercy* promised.... / He has *granted* that we'd be *rescued* ... / so that we could serve him without fear.... / Because of our God's deep compassion, / the dawn from heaven will break upon us, / to give light to those who are sitting in darkness / and in the shadow of death, / to guide us on the path of peace" (emphasis mine).

Does he care? Passionately!

In the room set aside for prayer that day, in the eerie silence where the only sounds were my knees creaking as I lowered myself to the floor and the twisting metal sound of a pulverized heart, I knelt at her feet as I imagined a professional mourner would. I didn't speak. How would that have helped? Instead, I entered into her grief with her, matching my mourning to the rhythm of hers. I breathed with her for a few moments.

Not until now, telling you this story, did it occur to me that's what happens when I grieve. Jesus kneels at my feet, holds my hand in his, and breathes in rhythm with my pain. And it is enough. For that moment.

While writing this chapter, I'm celebrating the end of a drought and a time of forced simplicity. Our house had been without water we could cook with, brush our teeth with, or drink for almost six months. It was a brutal winter. The brutality took out its fury on a portion of our well casing, causing a crack that still let a trickle of water into the house, but not *clean* water.

Here in the Northwoods, the frost plunged deep this past winter, preventing us from digging to the heart of the problem. The frost stayed long past its welcome. When spring arrived, it came with record-breaking rainfall that spaced itself out—bless its heart—so the yard was never dry enough for the backhoe to drive on, much less dig without threat of collapsing the trench. Add to that, five surgeries between my husband and me—most of them minor—in the same time period, and a husband who doesn't mind roughing it, and the equation spells month after month after month of filling jugs from the neighbor's well and brushing our teeth without running water.

Well into the summer, we were able to get the cracked portion replaced, went through the necessary process of purging the well of unwanted microorganisms, and could finally turn on the tap and take a nice long drink from what it offered.

A long, waterless stretch for people in a First World country.

We couldn't quit living, couldn't put life on hold, while we were without water. We made adjustments while we waited. And waited. And waited. The temporary crisis birthed a sensitivity in me for those whose drinking water isn't six months away but six miles—on foot—every day of their lives. My relatively small problem stirred a new compassion for those with a much larger water issue. I'm determined to see clean water provided to several villages in Third World countries.

That *new thing* developed in me while I was still in the middle of my story.

A fallow season? Not at all. Uncomfortable and inconvenient, but attitude-altering.

Silence before God or listening prayer is not fallow. It may cause discomfort initially, but it can lead to the kind of gratitude I felt when I could turn on a faucet and celebrate an unhindered flow of clear water. I listened. He sustained.

Most of the things that shatter a soul are far more serious than having to haul water from the neighbor's house for half a year.

God didn't hold back when he prompted Solomon to write, "He has made everything beautiful in its time. He has also set eternity in the human heart; yet no one can fathom what God has done from beginning to end" (Ecclesiastes 3:11 NIV).

Everything. All things. We can't imagine how that's possible in lives vandalized by abuse or torture. We see small glimpses in the artful stories of those who have repurposed their pain to warn, counsel, or rescue others. We see it in God's promise to rally to the needs of the defenseless. We hear it in the memoirs of Holocaust survivors who tell of individuals who risked everything to save a child or smuggle a crust of bread or demonstrate kindness in a horrific, hostile environment.

A young man emerged from years of trouble with the law and a life pockmarked with needle tracks and dangerous choices. Battered—and used to it—it surprised him to discover God was willing to breathe new life into his lungs, to redeem what seemed beyond all hope. The young man took baby steps, then giant steps, surrendering almost everything to the One who'd brought him back to life.

Almost everything.

A few blocks away, a young woman underwent a similar transformation, coached out of a routine of bad decisions with costly consequences. She too surrendered almost everything. Almost.

Before long, the two came to lean on one another.

And then it all fell apart. Dramatically.

Hopelessly? Even the optimistic wondered. The two had far less trouble abandoning themselves to old habits and unwise choices, to destructive relationship patterns and decisions that left God out of the picture than they did abandoning themselves fully to God.

The tentative peace the couple had tugged back from the precipice too many times disintegrated with a neighbor's frantic phone call to 911, the woman's trip to the emergency room to get checked out, and the man's trip to the city jail to get checked in.

What happened? Hope had gained a foothold. They'd made progress—noticeable progress—from their earlier addictions and string of bad decisions. They'd begun the mending process. What went wrong?

They used inferior material to mend the breach between them—each other. They depended on each other to fill the gaps. That's a task beyond any human's ability. The glue didn't hold. It has a short shelf life and grows brittle when exposed to adversity.

Can their relationship be repaired? Will their souls heal?

One of the quotes that recirculates through social media channels—author unknown—reads, "Bad chapters can still create a story that ends well. Let your past be a part of your story, not your identity."

The past kept intruding on the couple's present. Old ways of crisis management. Old methods of dealing with stress. Old habits of listening intently to the noise around them and avoiding the place of quieted waters.

Another couple spent themselves praying for their prodigal daughter. They'd thought *prodigal* meant "will come home eventually, repentant, and we'll be waiting," like the prodigal son in the Bible. Its academic definition is less hopeful than that. It means "reckless, particularly related to spending, wasteful, imprudent." And whatever definition the parents used, it didn't fit. Their daughter's recklessness had little to do with money, more to do with how she used her body and affections. And she didn't come home. She was buried without their knowledge by a county in another state. They found out years later. They'd still been praying for her return.

Where's the healing for them? Their daughter's gone. What they prayed for is no longer an option. And worse than that, she was taken from them before their family could be restored. What now? What can they expect? An endless ache?

In Hosea 2:15, speaking to those whose hearts had melted like this couple's, God said, "I will...make the Achor Valley a door of hope." A valley of trouble becomes a gateway to hope. The word *Achor* can be translated "gloomy, dejected." Those bearing heartaches that claw at the soul would use even stronger words than that to describe their pain.

Can hope show its face in that place?

We've seen it happen. We know it can. God promised it could. But too many of us don't know how to believe two things at once—that this hurts like fury, and yet God is telling the truth. Pain can become a door of hope.

Hope drew a deep breath for a friend. As a child, she'd been tortured by a community member who abused her in innumerable ways. As part of his torture and a prelude to other abuses, he often held her underwater until she passed out from lack of oxygen. Not surprisingly, she grew up with a crippling fear of water, especially the swimming she'd once loved. A swimming unit in gym class led to her missing an entire quarter of school. Summer outings at the lake kept her in a state of panic that someone would drag her to the water, thinking it funny. She bowed out of canoe trips and ferry rides. The water represented a terror she could not relive.

As an adult, the valley of desperation angered her enough that determination and a growing faith in the God of the impossible propelled her to the edge of the water. As if speaking to her long-gone abuser, she let the soles of her feet feel the water. Then waded in to ankle-depth, chanting, "You can't have this. You cannot have this."

The next day, she waded to her shaking knees, and survived.

She now swims recreationally and for exercise. Do the memories still surface? Yes. Every time she nears the edge of the pool or lake. But every time, she allows God to flood her with an uncommon courage and repeats, "You can't have this. You won't take this joy away from me." Lowering herself into the water and leaning back to float freely is an enormous victory no one else in the pool knows. But God sees. And applauds.

"Every lap I swim is a testimony to God's power to heal the unmendable," she insists. "Every time I get in the water, I'm drowning out the voice of the past and letting God do the talking."

I'm not practiced enough at letting God do the talking, at silent prayer, listening prayer. I've taken courses and read books and have become well-rehearsed in talking prayer. Asking prayer. Pleading prayer. Begging prayer. Let-me-tell-you-how-I-think-this-should-play-out-God prayer. But the silent variety? If there's an apprenticeship program for that, I'm in the early phase.

What I know so far is that mending has room to breathe in the space created by listening prayer. The mending I need. The mending others need if I grow quiet enough to relinquish my own ideas about how and when that should happen.

"There's a battle to be waged and fought for the survival of this art form," said Peter Gelb, General Manager of the New York City Metropolitan Opera, in an interview titled "The

Greatest Show on Earth" for the television show *60 Minutes.* He spoke of the art of opera. But we could say the same about the art form of mending through listening prayer.

It's a battle. But it's not a battle without a champion.

"God just doesn't throw a life preserver to a drowning person," wrote R. C. Sproul. "He goes to the bottom of the sea, and pulls a corpse from the bottom of the sea, takes him up on the bank, breathes into him the breath of life and makes him alive." And he nurtures us through the process of learning to value the healing virtues of silence.

A friend taught me that even talking prayer needs silence at the start—emptiness we create for God to fill with himself, with what artists and authors call "negative space" that complements, sets off, and frames prayer that has words.

Silent prayer is more silence than prayer. It listens, abandoned to a Voice that's rarely audible. The Voice takes our Dumpster full of broken, bent, awkwardly angled bits and reshapes them into works of fine art.

Who talks while we're engaged in prayerful silence? Jesus does.

I can trace one of the defining moments in my faith journey to the day I fully embraced the gift of Jesus' prayers for me. Me! Small and insignificant as I am in the scheme of things, tucked away between cornfields and cranberry bogs, plugging along with the simple tasks I've been called to do, with a name few but Jesus know. In a holy, inexplicable, never-anything-but-elegant way, he's pestering God the Father on my behalf!

And yours.

Romans 8:34 reminded me, "It is Christ Jesus who also pleads our case for us."

Hebrews 7:25 added the punctuation. "This is why [Jesus] can completely save those who are approaching God through him, because he always lives to speak with God for them." He *lives* for it.

Salvaged from a copper-roofed airport, metal scraps—that had served as rain collector, sun deflector, and landing pad for pigeon droppings—became gallery pieces.

As I listen intently, and use words only when necessary in prayer for people like my newly divorced friend and her young daughter, I'm watching the art emerge. What wrecked them doesn't have to destroy their value, their future, their hope.

Pigeons aren't allowed in galleries.

CHAPTER FIVE

TAPESTRY RESTORATION

Beauty in the Ragged

Even missing pieces tell a story.

A TATTERED SIXTEENTH-CENTURY ALTAR CLOTH became the object of attention for a panel of tapestry restoration experts. Upon early inspection, the needlework appeared crude. A rough edge gave the tapestry conservationists a clue that what they observed on the surface concealed an original piece much older, much more artistically crafted.

The top layer appeared to be an attempt to mend a frayed original version by replicating an earlier artisan's work. Would the team need to destroy the patch job—needlework from more than five hundred years ago—in order to reach the under layer presumed dating to the 1200s? If the under layer revealed irretrievable damage, would they regret losing one historical treasure in pursuit of the second?

What little they could see of the under layer showed exceptional craftsmanship. They took the risk and began the tedious work of—thread by thread—removing the amateur repair job to reveal fine details, delicate designs the coarse repair had hidden. A rare thirteenth-century artifact.

Faded? Yes. With areas so thin, the colored threads were gone in places, leaving only the inked outline of where the design had been. The inked outlines formed such a vital part of the story of the altar cloth that as the team mended other thin spots, they decided to leave the outlines untouched.

Have you ever assumed, like I have, that the only legitimate healing is complete healing? The only soul-mending that counts is eliminating the pain, fully restoring what was lost, reclaiming everything we once had? What if sometimes, rarely but sometimes, the outline of the hurt tells the story more effectively than if it were erased? Undetectable? No evidence we were ever wounded? What if?

A mother of a stillborn doesn't want to pretend she never had a child to lose. The invisible outline matters, despite its reminder of her grief. The veteran's limp reminds him how close he came to losing his life, but didn't.

A friend recently had a suspicious spot removed from her face. The surgeon plied his scalpel with an artist's hand. The spot was benign. But my friend is left with a two-inch scar that makeup can only partially disguise. Her attitude is admirable. When she looks in the mirror, the natural tendency would be to notice the mar. She rejoices with, "It was benign!"

The medical community tells us scar tissue forms when a tatter or rip, an abrasion or puncture, injures the skin below the outer surface. It's the body's natural response to help repair the breach—to bridge the gap left by the injury. The final stage of healing is the formation of a scar.

No scar is inherently beautiful. But it can be perceived as beautiful because of what it represents.

"I lived through that!"

"That happened to me and I'm still alive to tell about it?"

An antique lover will run a hand over the depressions in a two-hundred-year-old cutting board and marvel at the stories each scar could relate. Or see the divots in a wooden high chair tray and imagine the teething babies who tested its edges. Or smile over fingerprints left on a long-buried artifact. Or find charming the wooden spool replacing a cupboard's original knob. Or purchase the *Little House on the Prairie* slant-topped desk because of the scars carved into its surface. The scars have stories to tell.

Wounds demand immediate attention. They're susceptible to infection. They leave the spot vulnerable to reinjury. A scar forms a protective barrier, even when it isn't pretty.

Scars gone crazy or located in the wrong place can become adhesions or cause undue pain. But scars form a stronger protection than new skin alone.

A thirteenth-century tapestry reminds us that what's under the scar, even raw, tells an important story.

– – – – –

A soul's mending is rarely if ever linear. It doesn't follow a strict time line or a smooth incline. As with grief, despite predictions, the process can take much longer than anyone imagined. And it will dip and sway, rush along then bog down, inch forward then settle into a place of not mere acceptance but peace.

Many of us can track the progress of our healing by the puckered tearstains on the pages of our Bible or the dog-eared edges of a treasured photograph.

Where's the art in that? It's messy. Destructive in some ways. But still art. The messes lie on the floor, smeared on the palette, on the easel, around the potter's wheel, on the sewing room floor—bits and snips, selvage edges that don't work into a polished finished product, loose threads, ends, and knots.

It's an imperfect metaphor, but it's also a call to those of us who thought we had to discard something—a relationship, a piece of ourselves—because of an unsightly tear in an important spot, a missing piece. Can it become a work others reference to find hope for their soul's tapestry?

Our surviving what we're dumped into or what frays our soul necessitates creativity. A neutral position breeds stagnation, which breeds disease, depression, and the stench of death. It's as true in the human heart as it is in the backwaters of a creek, an ignored splinter, or an untended wound.

My brothers and sisters and their spouses gathered with children and grandchildren last November to reconnect, to celebrate Thanksgiving, and to wrap our arms around my sister-in-law who was between chemo appointments.

She brought pumpkin bars.

We'd made it clear she didn't have to bring anything. The rest of us—those without a cancer battle—would provide the meal. She insisted because serving made her feel more normal. And serving mends tattered souls.

Days ahead of her and days behind her proved too taxing. But when she could, throughout her cancer journey, she served because she understood serving's inherent healing properties.

Serving coaxes us away from the natural self-absorption of pain's cliff edge.

Galatians 5:13—"Serve each other through love."

First Peter 4:10—"And serve each other according to the gift each person has received, as good managers of God's diverse gifts."

Serving our way to a place of soul-healing.

Rescuing an abandoned dog because you once needed rescuing. Adopting because you waited too long to be adopted, and you know how that feels. Taking flowers to someone else's graveside near your friend's or loved one's because that person's memory never receives the honor. Raising money for the children's cancer ward because you no longer have a child who needs its services.

Think about the images that leave the strongest impact on the human heart. An American soldier arching his body over a child in harm's way as the shrapnel rains. Self-sacrifice makes it beautiful.

The businessman who removes his shoes for the destitute man with none. Still a tattered scene. Grace makes it beautiful.

The octogenarian husband settling his dying wife into his arms for her last breaths. Still heartbreaking. Love makes it beautiful.

The abuse victim summoning courage to tell her story so others can be spared. Still shattered. Courage makes it beautiful.

The widow who volunteers as a peer counselor. Still grieving. Selflessness makes it beautiful.

An athlete stopping to offer himself as a brace to help an injured competitor across the finish line. Humility makes it beautiful.

The most artful images are so often those of people serving one another, helping each other get through it.

Did you see the gone-viral portrait of three Oklahoma girls—ages three, six, and four—all cancer patients, captured by photographer Lora Scantling? They stood in a pose of community and caring in the middle of their treatment protocols. Balded-headed, but dressed in elegant boutique lace, organza, and pearls, the girls embraced in a grip that said to the world, "Sometimes strength comes from knowing that you are not alone." Such tenderness and beauty are captured in that image and on those fragile but fierce faces!

In the middle of their battles, the art in their expressions and their embrace journeyed around the world to bring awareness to childhood cancer and hope to those who felt it impossible to find anything of worth, anything artistic in the middle of their own stories.

I find it pause-worthy that the photographer now reports each of the little girls is either in remission or cured as of this writing. But the impact they made—the resonance of their story—came during their battle for healing.

Don't we too often believe that we're worthless until we're mended? That while broken, we have nothing to offer? That all the wonder lies on the other side of healing?

You're holding this book in your hands, and are this far into its chapters, drawn to this mending place because of what you're bearing, what you've borne, or out of concern for those around you whose shattered lives grip your heart. You too are invested in moving past resignation of the tattered state of the soul, family, relationships, emotions, faith. You want to believe wholeness is possible. You need to believe it.

Centuries ago, a man came to Jesus with a shredded soul. His heartbreak? A son who from childhood had been tormented by seizures, and by a spirit of self-destruction, mute-ness, and deafness. Imagine watching your son on such a suicidal path that he would throw himself into a fire or into water to self-harm in response to his internal anguish. Imagine trying to protect the child from himself. Imagine years of family life with that concern center stage.

All too easy to speculate?

Did the man have other children? Where was his wife—home with the rest of their offspring? Home with a migraine? Insane over her grief?

The story opens with a large crowd gathered around the man and his boy—arguing. Arguing. Religious and legal experts and some of those following Jesus engaged in hot debate among themselves and with—or about—the shattered man and his son. That's all the father needed. To have the community pointing fingers and offering advice and, no doubt, making comments like, "Can't you keep that boy at home? He's so disruptive!"

The disciples wanted to help, but couldn't. It seemed a challenge greater than those they'd encountered before, although other deaf people had been healed in their presence, the blind suddenly sighted, thousands fed from one sack lunch, storms stilled, the tortured set free from their demons…

But this case. This one. Too hard.

So the father found himself embroiled in a discussion with people who didn't get it. They didn't understand what daily life was like with a self-destructive son. They didn't understand the depth of the dad's love, either. Or his persistence when every normal and several abnormal paths had been tried. Still no healing for the broken places deep in the son's—and the father's—souls.

Jesus steps onto the scene. "What are you arguing about?"

The man came forward, his face likely twisted in pain at having to describe yet again what was wrong with his son and how even those who followed Jesus had been unable to bring peace to the situation.

Jesus never listened to a heart cry like that and walked away, disinterested. Ever. He invited the man to bring his son to him.

The father said, "If you can do anything, help us! Show us compassion!" (Mark 9:22).

Please don't miss this artistry. The father didn't plead, "Help him. Show him compassion." He said, "Help us." He boldly acknowledged that his son's condition affected the whole family. Freeing his son from the torturous thoughts and actions would free the whole family.

Caregiver, husband, friend, mother, father, wife, daughter, son of a fractured soul, God's invitation to mend encompasses the whole family. His healings always affect more than the individual in the epicenter of the distress. Concentric circles of mending radiate out from that center, touching—sometimes—a whole community. Our serving others while in the process shows others that mending is possible. And stunning.

In the story of the father with a tortured son, Jesus responded, "If? If I can do anything about it?" We know from other passages that Jesus is moved with compassion by our grief and sorrow. That knowledge informs our understanding of what his tone of voice might have been like in that interchange. His question may have been the father's first real sign of hope. It's as if Jesus were saying to this exhausted father, "Ask me something hard." Tendrils of healing must have danced their way through the father's soul at that moment, touching raw nerve endings with an inexplicable balm.

"All things are possible for the one who has faith," Jesus added.

The father wanted to believe. Wanted to believe his broken son could be whole, their tattered family, whole. The father didn't whisper, he cried out, "I have faith; help my lack of faith!" (Mark 9:24).

Braver than we are, the man confessed, "I have a measure of faith. That's why I'm here. But then I look at my son, hear his incoherent screams, think back on all the cures we've tried, relive the nightmares. I look around at all the people in as much trouble as we are and wonder why you would care to intervene for us. I believe, Jesus. Wherever my faith is frayed, make it whole!"

All of the man's prayers were answered. Even the risky prayer for greater faith, for pulling back another layer to find the treasure underneath. His son was freed, the community awed, their family restored.

The father-son relationship must have seemed like it was starting over, from a place unencumbered by fear. Daily schedules changed. Peace replaced chaos. They could finally reach out to help others, once the focus was lifted from their constant chaos.

Peace and mending. How beautifully interchangeable!

The burn scars on the young man's body no longer spoke of torment but of a previous chapter of his life—an earlier era—before a touch from Jesus. Imagination makes us wonder how the father's arms could have escaped being burned and scarred from his incessant, desperate act of pulling his son from the flames. Were the father's sear marks healed too?

And if a nightmare resurfaced? Or a wave of fear caused the father to hold his breath, waiting for seizures that never came? He—and we—turn to an essential truth like this one:

> Whenever I feel my foot slipping,
>> your faithful love steadies me, LORD.
> When my anxieties multiply,
>> your comforting calms me down.
> —Psalm 94:18-19

The cry never really ceases for any of us. "I believe. Help my lack of faith."

CHAPTER SIX

FINE ART RECLAMATION

A Meticulous Mend

We can't disturb the signature. It's his work, not ours.
—Art restoration expert

THE SCENE OPENED WITH A TATTERED, WATER-spotted, battered-in-places canvas painting hundreds of years old. Once demanding a high price, it lay lifeless on the worktable. Where the canvas had been folded, dried paint had cracked and fallen away. Brushstrokes centuries old were interrupted by the vulgarities of mistreatment. Had it been stuffed in a closet? Hidden from an encroaching army? Assumed worthless and packed away in a basement with other dusty, moldy things?

The passion in the narrator's voice held me captive as I watched an online video from the Art Conservation Department at Buffalo State College. The restoration expert talked for a few minutes about the process of restoring oil paintings created by master artists. I watched as the video revealed scenes of the painstaking cleaning process—small stroke after small stroke with a soft brush or swab—before restoration could advance. Thread-by-thread repair of canvas damage. Meticulous color mixing and research of ancient pigments to match the original as closely as possible.

The restoration artist used the kind of magnifying eyeglasses a neurosurgeon might use, alternating with a high-powered microscope for even finer work. She mimicked the original artist's brushstrokes, sometimes with a brush as fine as a single hair. One of the difficulties, she said, was the area around the artist's signature. "We can't disrupt the signature of the artist," she insisted as the piece of art stirred to life again.

The restoration expert on the video made several poignant statements I couldn't help but apply to the Divine Invitation for us to join God in mending the damaged artwork of the human soul. In her lyrical accent, the restorer said, "Of course, you grow attached to the object you're treating. You spend many hours with it and get to know it intimately. You're handling it with your own hands. You're looking at it from so up close. You're almost kissing the painting."

She spoke of the intense research needed before starting the process of restoring a damaged piece of artwork, investigating the history of the painting and the techniques of the artist, what materials might have originally been used. The restorer emphasized the importance of knowing the artist and the artist's work.

"It's not my work. It's his," she said. And she pointed again to the artist's signature.

"Of course you grow attached during the soul-healing process," we could echo. We spend hours with the Divine Restorer and get to know him intimately. We're looking at The Healer from "so up close." He's almost kissing the soul that needs mending.

It's not our work. The soul wasn't our invention. It was his.

I lingered over that concept and replayed the video to hear the line again. "We can't disrupt the signature of the artist."

As our souls mend, or as we walk alongside others in their mending processes, the methods we use and the brush of thoughts can never disrupt the signature of the Artist, or the piece is ruined. The goal is to restore the piece as nearly as possible to what it looked like in the mind of the artist before the denigration, deterioration, water spots, and wear. Before the sun damage, the smoke and soot from oil lamps or coal furnaces in homes and galleries where the paintings once hung. Before the abuse that raked rough nails across a soul's surface, or the battering of a thousand hailstones of neglect.

Damage to a priceless oil painting breaks the hearts of those who care about fine art. The restorer moves beyond a broken heart to the meticulous work of mending.

Too often we fear we can advance no farther than heart-broken. The idea had been pounded into my friend "Kari's" head, disrupting the signature of the One who created her.

Kari's childhood reinforced her parents' and community's pronouncement that she'd never succeed at anything. "Poor thing just doesn't have it in her," they said. Within earshot.

"The idea that I was destined for failure was drilled into me over and over again. Not surprisingly, nothing ever worked out the way I had planned. Maybe Robert Frost was right. There were two roads and I consistently took the wrong one. I eventually moved out of my parents' house to attend college, much to everyone's surprise."

I could feel the sting in her words as she gathered courage to tell me more.

"During my junior year, I fell in love and never finished my fourth year. It figured. So typical for me. I'd never succeed at anything. But I was bound and determined to succeed in this relationship, even though I wondered if I was doing the right thing. I got married despite my friends and family on both sides questioning if he was the right one for me.

"We all come into a relationship with baggage," Kari said. "For me that baggage was strapped with failure and a lack of acceptance. I was looking for love. Did I find it? No."

So far, Kari's story sounded like far too many I'd heard.

"After five children, a month before our twenty-fifth wedding anniversary my husband decided enough was enough and left. The past years have been hard. But they forced me to find me. I discovered I'm not as bad as I thought I was. I can do things. And I am an overcomer. I found the love I was missing in an intimate relationship with Jesus Christ that radically changed my perception of who I was and where I should look for answers to questions about my worth."

Bravo, Kari!

"Do I struggle?" she asked. "Absolutely. Before, I always succumbed to the fear of failure and not feeling I could thrive. I used to think I was beyond repair, that my brokenness couldn't be mended.

"The day my husband left me, I was alone with a teenage son still depending on me. It would have been so easy to bury my head under the covers and not face reality. But with God's help I have worked hard to find me, and I'm thriving. I finished my bachelor's degree. My master's degree will be completed this year. I started my own business that is slowly growing. The old Kari couldn't have done this. If I can start over, so can anyone else."

The body's natural inclination is to heal, barring infection, misuse, reinjury, or secondary issues. Even though the process of healing naturally takes longer as a person ages, all body systems rally to assist healing of an injury. White blood cells rush to the site. Heart rate may increase, to pump more blood.

The soul's natural inclination is to heal from trauma, too. It was created by the Artisan to embrace the process of mending. We see it from an in utero infant to the octogenarian with a new hip.

Barring infection, misuse, reinjury, or secondary issues.

People can sabotage the healing process when they reinfect the soul's wound with toxic choices. They submit themselves to reinjury when they refuse to distance themselves from the pathological abuser, or walk into a sanity-threatening environment unguarded. They can halt the healing when they focus all their attention on it, making it the centerpiece of their lives.

Healing grows best away from the glare of fluorescents and the heat of spotlights, in the quiet of "still waters," which God tells us is the preferred environment for restoring our soul, as we're told in Psalm 23.

He. "*He* restores my soul." The Twenty-third is one of the psalms written from a place of deep soul-distress—from the heart of a man bullied, pursued by enemies, falsely accused, threatened with death, abandoned by those who called him a friend. David suffered bouts of depression and self-doubt. But he acknowledged that God's intention is to restore, to mend tattered souls. We're not seeking God's aid for something he's disinclined to do. Those who seek refuge in him find it.

David the psalmist, the warrior, the leader, the writer lived life keenly aware of his mortality, his vulnerability, and the condition of his soul.

"Why, my soul, are you downcast? / Why so disturbed within me?" he asked. Frequently. We see that question in Psalm 42:5 (NIV) and 11, and again in Psalm 43:5. The Common English Bible gives us a little more insight into what that expression means in today's vernacular. "Why, I ask myself, are you so depressed? / Why are you so upset inside?" His soul was in need of mending. And he knew it.

We toss around the word *soul* as if it needs no explanation.

"Let my whole being [my soul] bless the Lord!" reads Psalm 103:1. Psalm 103:1-2 in the New Century Version words it this way: "All that I am, praise the Lord; / everything in me, praise his holy name. / My whole being, praise the Lord / and do not forget all his kindnesses."

When a soul is tattered, shredded, we understand how the word *soul* encompasses our whole being. Everything in us. What isn't affected? Appetite is. Sleep. Enjoyment of simple pleasures. Time. Energy. Ability to cope with stressors we once surfed. Health. Vitality. Essence. Relationships.

Life seems to revolve around our pain. Anything good or productive we accomplish is a monumental victory over the all-encompassing sorrow. And monumentally exhausting.

Soul—the intangible "who we are."

The Hebrew expression of soul—*nephesh* or *nepesh*—as used in the Old Testament connotes "vitality in all of its breadth and width of meaning," according to Christian Wolf's observations from the *Holman Bible Dictionary*.

When an event or circumstance leaves our soul tattered, we're affected to the core of our vitality, our very life. Who would expect an injury reaching that deep to be healed with "There, there now" or a cartoon-character Band-Aid?

But where can we find the equivalent of quiet—or as some commentaries express it—*quieted* waters?

My children are grown. I work at home. My husband likes to stay busy with outdoor activities. And it still isn't easy to find quieted waters where God can restore my soul.

Have you seen an immersion blender at work? It's the culinary equivalent of a handheld boat motor pulverizing sauces and gravies. Some days, life sticks its blades into the quiet waters and churns them like an immersion blender. If the churning were due to unnecessary or frivolous activities, I'd know the solution. Click the off switch.

What if the churning can't be categorized as wasted time or a worthless pursuit? What if the activities that keep life from quieting seem—on the surface at least—mandatory?

What if the soul shredding is the very thing keeping us from that place of quiet where it can mend?

Where's the quiet place in a round-the-clock vigil in the ICU family waiting room? Is it the hospital chapel? A few stolen moments between visits and the tasks related to keeping the long-distance family informed?

Where's a safe place for restoring souls in the women's

shelter among the traumatized? Yes, the shelter provides a temporary refuge. Is temporary long enough for mending?

How can our soul find restoration when the room is quiet but our mind won't stop chattering, arguing with us about the hopelessness of our situation?

God's invitation to mend isn't prefaced with, "If at all possible," "If you can fit it into your schedule," "If you have nothing else to do," "If you have some time on your hands."

He restores my soul in the midst of the chaos. He nudges me toward a pocket of spiritual quiet during the crisis, not when it's all over. He may use a park, or that chapel, or an art gallery or concert or worship experience. Or he may plant me in a chair in the family room with no television noise, no radio, no smartphone in my hand.

He may quiet the waters as I dive into the pages of a book that seems to express my heart, or that soundlessly rehearses the character qualities of The Mender until I finally understand. He may lead me to poetry with a rhythm that stills the waters before the words land against the shore. Or it may be the view from my kitchen window that draws my thoughts away from the chaos to a place of calm.

Why does healing thrive in stillness? Especially in the stillness we have to fight for, plan for, sacrifice for?

Commotion agitates wounds. Commotion keeps our thoughts centered on doing, achieving, striving. Stillness is often a prelude to surrender. In surrender—not to the pain, but to The Healer—we abandon ourselves to the process, to the One whose steady hand pieces the ripped canvas back together, thread by thread.

There's an intimacy in quietness that is distinct from other ways of connecting with God. "In quietness and confidence is your strength," he assures us in Isaiah 30:15 NLT. "Let all the earth be silent before him," reads Habakkuk 2:20.

Psalm 62:1 says, "I wait quietly before God, / for my victory comes from him" (NLT). Verse 5 of that chapter adds another layer onto the concept: "Let all that I am wait quietly before God, / for my hope is in him." All that I am. My soul.

The quieted soul invites healing. The agitated soul tears at the sutures. The stitches. Smudges the paint repairs. Quiet helps create a climate-controlled environment for optimal healing.

I'm more alert now for the quiet places. Like an antique buff watching for the familiar sign or a knitter drawn to a yarn shop or a fisherman who recognizes a bait shop from half a mile away, I'm on the alert for pockets of quiet where God can restore my soul.

CHAPTER SEVEN

NEEDLEWORK REPAIR

Recaptured Wholeness

A snag. A hole. Ruin.
A needle. Wool. Whole.

FOR SEVERAL YEARS, I WORKED PART-TIME FOR A
world-renowned knitter and knitting craft expert. I found it
impossible not to fall in love with wool, with circular knitting
techniques, with the mystery of color patterns and storied
history of the art form. Her studio smelled of sheepswool
lanolin and books and creativity.

The knitting expert refused to even mouth the word *moth*,
but instead spelled it with a missing letter, like someone

avoiding the crassness of a four-letter word: M_TH. I carried a m_th-eaten project of my own to her, mourning what I assumed was the loss of the handcrafted sweater. She looked at the jagged hole and asked if I'd saved any matching wool from the project. I had, a lesson I'd learned early in my employment/infatuation with knitting.

She threaded a large-gauge darning needle with a rounded rather than sharp point and meticulously retraced the pattern the stitches would have made if not for the m_th. She wove the needle in and out, recreating what had been lost, exactly mimicking the tension and spacing of the intact stitches that remained. The darning needle did the looping/connecting work knitting needles had originally accomplished. Like an explorer following an intricate map, the knitter stayed focused on the task until eventually the sweater was presented back to me—whole, useable again, repaired so skillfully I couldn't detect where the hole had once been.

It took an expert, an artist. But as I watched, she taught me—a novice—how to mend. The skill has proven itself valuable countless times since then. Where her fingers moved elegantly, knowingly, to repair the damage, mine move more stiffly. Occasionally I have to unravel what I've done and try again. But I now know a garment I assume is garbage can almost always be salvaged.

The creative genius, God, is not intimidated by the magnitude of the repair needed. He's never stumped for an idea of how to make art out of the ugliness in our lives. Even the unspeakable ugliness or soul-gouging that crossed your mind just now.

This is the God to whom we entrust ourselves for the mending process. This genius God who turns a knobby, shapeless rhizome into a lace-edge iris, a wrinkled brown seed into a morning glory, and the ripping pain of childbirth into a cause for celebration.

"There is no beauty here," said the woman seated next to me in the plane. Her brother lay in a medically induced coma until the family could gather. The doctor's last option was a procedure with two possible outcomes—death or a little improvement. If the procedure succeeded, they'd try bringing him out of the coma. That, too, had opposing potential outcomes. He'd lived alone for decades. Half the family hadn't spoken to him since the battle over their mother's estate. They may not have a chance.

The sister in the seat next to me breathed as if the seat belt compressed her chest, not her lap.

"Does he know you love him, that you care?"

A faint smile softened the expression on her face. "We spoke the day before his stroke. Yes, he knows."

That moment represented a bead of hope threaded onto the unraveled sleeve of their broken family. Her reaching the hospital in time would add another. His resurrection from the coma, another bead. Adequate time for the family to heal, another.

I pictured the snagged cuffs of the sweater she wore laced with small, bright glass beads representing tiny, hope-filled moments. I pray her sleeves are now weighted with elegant strands, jewelry where the ragged edges had been.

An online image of an unraveled sleeve captured my attention. I enlarged the image to examine the intricate design that had repaired a once-tattered edge. An artisan had used 14-carat gold thread to sew a series of French knots to keep the sleeve from unraveling further and to defy broken with exquisitely beautiful. I'm looking at worn edges with new eyes these days.

My college roommate's daughter, Jessica, was asked to examine a blanket a friend had crocheted for her wedding more than a decade earlier. The ten-plus years of love had left the blanket shabby, and not in a shabby-chic way. It sported a huge hole that grew larger every time the blanket saw use.

The value lay in what the blanket symbolized—the beginning days of their marriage. The hope of a lifetime together.

Jessica, a self-taught expert at fiber arts, knew it was no small project to tackle, but agreed to see if the keepsake could be repaired.

The yarn had dulled over the years from its once vibrant sheen. The hole—the size of an adult hand—made the blanket unusable. As Jessica examined the hole, she realized yarn ends had come loose and started a chain reaction of unraveling, with long loops of yarn hanging from the edges of the abyss, stretched and worn.

Jessica took the wedding keepsake home with her, spread the blanket on her living room floor, and carefully aligned the intact stitches to make sense of what was missing. So much was gone. The pattern wasn't complicated, but a simple patch wouldn't work.

"A normal crochet project," she said, "only involves working into the stitches below. Fixing this hole meant I needed to work into the stitches below *and* the stitches above. I wasn't making something new, so I didn't have the freedom to do it the easy way. I was fixing something old, so I had to work within the structure someone else had already made."

Reading her description rocked me with its similarities to mending a tattered soul.

"Stitch by stitch, I saw the pattern reforming between my

fingers," Jessica wrote. "A few inches in, and it became difficult to tell which stitches were my repairs, and which were the original work. When I was finished, the blanket still looked love-worn. But it was whole. Strong enough to endure the next half-century of their marriage.

"I consider having saved that homemade blanket, meticulous as the process was, one of the most satisfying projects I've ever worked on," she said. "To take something broken and make it unbroken? It was as if some very small part of the universe rang true again."

Such delicate work. No wonder repairs to the human soul take longer than we imagine they will. It's delicate, painstaking, many-layered work.

When the surgeon operating on my son-in-law's cervical vertebrae took his time, those of us in the waiting room didn't complain. The surgeon's instruments came within a hair's breadth of nerves that—if nicked—could have turned my son-in-law into a quadriplegic. The team would advance, then were forced to retreat and wait while a hot spot of nerves settled down so they could move forward again. Exacting, meticulous, intricate work. More long hours in the recovery area. Finally the word came, "He's moving his fingers and toes."

His healing took months before he was free of the metal neck brace. Even now, his movements are moderately restricted. No more reaching above his head with a paint-brush. No more climbing on roofs or carrying sections of tree trunks on his shoulder. No more wrestling.

But he's restored. Those concessions seem small compared to what might have been the outcome if the medical community hadn't discovered that his spinal column was pinched to the thinness of a ribbon, and if they hadn't used a cautious, however-much-time-it-takes approach to the surgery.

Sometimes mending a threadbare soul or reweaving the unraveled becomes a more complex issue because of the layers of impact. I'm awed by what I'm just now—after all these years—seeing in the outlying edges of many of the stories recorded in Scripture.

Who was impacted when Jesus turned two loaves and five small fish into enough to feed five thousand men plus women and children? Those with growling stomachs? So many more than that.

Relationally, what happened? Think of what the gift of food did for the woman who hadn't thought to pack a lunch that day for her children. Think of how she was spared the sharp tongue of her impatient husband's ridicule. Think of the embarrassed man without the funds to hire someone to bring food for his family, or the friends who cared about the needy but had no means with which to meet the need.

Hungry stomachs temporarily filled—merely a side benefit to the depth of what happened relationally and spiritually when Jesus intervened.

Nothing God the Father or his Son Jesus did had only a single layer of impact.

Consider the oil pots that never ran dry until a debt was paid (2 Kings 4). An answer to a destitute widow's prayer. It happened in front of her sons, who couldn't help but learn about a God who provides even when a family is caught in impossible circumstances.

I paused just now to let that soak into my own empty places.

The widow's boys would have been taken as slaves to pay what was owed had God not intervened. A debt paid? Provision enough for their future? A blessing. The woman's sons' lives spared, the family intact? Priceless.

The Bible tells another story through the eyes of a rich young woman from Shunem. She'd been kind to Elisha and his servant when they traveled through the area where she and her much older husband lived. She'd provided a guest room for them whenever they needed it. In response, Elisha asked if there were something she wanted them to request of the king on her behalf. The humble woman replied that she was content (2 Kings 4:13). No needs.

A brave statement. She had no son. In that culture, when her aging husband died, she would be alone, ostracized as too many widows were, and without ongoing protection or provision. With no offspring to carry on the family name or legacy.

She'd asked for nothing. But the prophet promised she'd hold a son in her arms within the year. Her response shows that despite her outward bravery, she had a deep longing she hadn't voiced. "Please don't raise my hopes" (4:28).

How many infertility doctors have heard a similar brokenhearted plea? "Don't tell me this is possible if it isn't."

But almost a year later, the woman from Shunem held a newborn son in her arms.

The child grew. The Bible tells us that one day he ran to his father who was overseeing the harvest workers in his fields. The boy clutched his head, crying out in pain.

The father made a decision he might forever regret. He didn't attend to the boy's needs himself. He stayed with the harvesters and sent one of his workers to take the distressed boy to his mother.

The boy sat in his mother's lap while she comforted him, unable to do anything to relieve his pain. The boy died at noon. She laid him on the bed in the guest room and left the house to find the man of God, Elisha. She told her husband nothing about what had happened, even when he asked where she was going. It's curious the father didn't ask how his son was doing.

Fast-forwarding, we see the prophet Elisha coming to the child's side and performing a holy version of CPR. The boy's life was restored. The woman's future restored. The family legacy reclaimed.

A historical event dripping with poignancy. A healing with far-reaching, deeply layered impact.

"Why is my soul mend taking so long?" we might ask.

Because it's about so much more than one thing. And because the process itself is part of the healing.

In 2 Kings 8, we see another layer of what began with the Shunamite woman's hospitality in providing a guest room, asking nothing in return. From the wording, it appears her elderly husband had died. She was the head of the household now. Elisha warned her to leave the area because of an approaching famine predicted to last seven years. She obeyed, taking her son and her household to Philistia to ride out the famine.

When she returned, she approached the king to appeal for her house and farmland.

She'd humbly asked nothing of the king years ago. Now, she needed his favor to restore the property she'd had to abandon. At the moment she stood before the king, the prophet's servant was in conversation with him about that very thing. God had sent someone ahead of her to pave the way for the discussion that would result in the return of everything that belonged to her, including all the harvest the fields had produced in the seven years she was gone.

We wonder if all we can expect is to survive. Our brokenness feels like a permanent condition. When God mends, he provides so much more than mere survival.

And it sometimes takes years for the whole story to unfold. Detailed planning on God's part. Humility on ours.

In the meantime? In the middle?

We play the soundtrack that holds our thoughts in alignment with healing, as a knitter might hold a damaged piece straight while she tackles the repair work. A soundtrack of worship.

"Would you like to choose the music?" the MRI technician asked me as he strapped me to the table that would slide me into the Dome of the Unknown. I knew better than to refuse the offer of music. It wasn't my first MRI. At the time—technology may have improved before this book reaches you—the machine sounded like a jackhammer when it performed its imaging.

"Yes, music. Please. Do you have anything...worshipful?"

"Absolutely." He pushed the button that transported me deeper into the machine. I'd learned the last time that if I kept my eyes closed, I could trick my brain into thinking there was more space between my face and the interior of the dome.

"How's that level?" the hollow intercom voice asked as music surrounded me.

I heard the strains of one of my favorite songs about God My Healer, all I need. "Better crank it up."

Worship silences noise. It drowns out the sound of the dentist's drill and the hammering of our adrenalin-fired heartbeat. Worship transforms the moans of a wounded soul into a sound that reverberates through us, and through the halls of heaven.

One of the most beautiful and artistic healing sounds in history—especially of interest to those whose *souls* are tattered—was the sound of fabric tearing in the temple in Jerusalem the moment Jesus died. We're told in the Bible that a heavy curtain separated the Holy of Holies—symbolic for the separation between humanity and the holiness of God. At the crucifixion, the curtain was torn from top to bottom, as if God's hands held the top edge and pulled the fabric apart to allow us access, the intimacy we never could have known if it weren't for the death of Jesus on our behalf.

The sound of torn fabric became praise music the world could dance to.

Torn souls became evidence of divine art.

–   –   –   –   –

David, the psalmist, had a man cave. Not by choice. By necessity. Relentlessly pursued by longtime enemies, and by an army led by a betrayer-friend, David and his followers retreated to the caves at Adullum. More than once.

It was from that fortification, that hiding place, that he wrote many of the psalms. The poetry and journaling of his personal healing were written under duress. Those psalms, which have become a soundtrack for our own mending, were written from a pulverized soul. It's breath-stealing, isn't it? The beauty, the art, of what was created in the bowels of darkness!

I'm sure there were times the suffocating interior of those deep caves at Adullum were inky dark for David and his men. But from them came:

> Have mercy on me, God;
>> have mercy on me
>> because I have taken refuge in you.
>> I take refuge
>> in the shadow of your wings
>>> until destruction passes by.
>> (Psalm 57:1)

And this:

>> I cry out loud for help from the LORD.
>>> I beg out loud for mercy from the LORD.
>> I pour out my concerns before God;
>>> I announce my distress to him.
>> When my spirit is weak inside me, you still know
>>> my way.
>>> But they've hidden a trap for me in the path
>> I'm taking.
>>> Look right beside me: See?
>>> No one pays attention to me.
>>> There's no escape for me.
>>> No one cares about my life. (Psalm 142:1-4)

Did David have his finger on the pulse of the raked-raw human heart? It started with his own. From the midst of the darkness, he felt the tug of needle and thread on his shattered soul. He sensed the tender yet strong embrace of the God who had promised his protection despite how external circumstances appeared. So David concluded that psalm with:

I cry to you, LORD, for help.

"You are my refuge," I say.

"You are all I have in the land of the living."

Pay close attention to my shouting,

Because I've been brought down so low!

Deliver me from my oppressors

because they're stronger than me.

Get me out of this prison

so I can give thanks to your name.

Then the righteous will gather all around me

because of your good deeds to me.

(Psalm 142:5-7)

How could we doubt that his "mending in the dark" times informed and inspired other psalms he wrote? Like this one:

Save me, God,

because the waters have reached my neck!

I have sunk into deep mud.

My feet can't touch the bottom!

I have entered deep water;

The flood has swept me up.

I am tired of crying

My throat is hoarse.

> My eyes are exhausted with waiting for my
> God. (Psalm 69:1-3)

And these words:

> You know full well the insults I've received;
>> you know my shame and my disgrace.
> All my adversaries are right there in front of
>> you.
> Insults have broken my heart.
>> I'm sick about it.
> I hoped for sympathy,
>> but there wasn't any;
>> I hoped for comforters,
>> but couldn't find any. (Psalm 69:19-20)

And this passage:

> You who seek God—
> let your hearts beat strong again
>> because the Lord listens to the needy
>> and doesn't despise his captives.
>
> Let heaven and earth praise God,
> the oceans too, and all that moves within them!
> (Psalm 69:32-34)

Those familiar with the psalms notice a telling pattern that marks almost every one. Whether written by David or one of the other songwriters, they may begin with a desperate cry for help, but end with worship. During the process of spilling out his brokenness, David's focus moved from his pain to his Hope.

When David and his men emerged from the caves to return to battle, what had changed? The strategies of the enemy? No. Had David's problems suddenly disappeared, the threats vanished? No.

Nothing had changed except his soul's fortification. And that was enough.

Even beyond the *words* or lyricism of the psalms, that *pattern* speaks to us, especially when we're attempting to mend in the dark. A pattern of honesty before God, vulnerability, and a return to praise.

Another of David's psalms became the song I clung to when my heart sank to the cave floor at the sudden loss of my father. I held the phone receiver in my hand as I sat in the dark hallway of the home I was visiting when I heard the news. My hostess sat and cried with me, then left me alone as I requested. With the news still stinging and soul scraping, I eventually retreated to the guest room and sprawled across the bed, listening to the distant train and my mind's replay of everything I would miss about him. Lying there on the cave floor, breathing the choking dust of pummeled rock, I heard the words that have become a go-to source of renewal in the darkness:

> God, listen to my cry;
>> pay attention to my prayer!
> When my heart is [overwhelmed],
>> I cry out to you from the very ends of the
>> earth.
> Lead me to the rock that is higher than I am
>> because you have been my refuge,
>> a tower of strength. (Psalm 61:1-3)

"When my heart is overwhelmed, Lord, lead me to the rock that is higher than I."

From the cave-prison where David the psalmist hid from his pursuers, he wrote songs that formed part of his life's personal soundtrack.

> My heart, O God, is steadfast,
>> my heart is steadfast;
>> I will sing and make music.
> Awake, my soul! (Psalm 57:7-8 NIV)

David understood the difference between his spirit—which would live with God forever; his body—which would eventually die like everyone else's; and his soul—his mind, will, and emotions.

His tattered soul composed songs of worship that accompanied his journey back to wholeness.

David knew his mind, will, and emotions didn't always track with what he knew in his spirit. All three layers needed alignment. All three needed reminders, fortification, and comfort.

My worship soundtrack is loaded with psalms and other worship songs that have accompanied my journey. I "hear" their melodies when I read their lyrics. I let them wash over me when the radio brings one to mind. I stop what I'm doing and lean back in my office chair, eyes closed, heart open, when I recall a psalm that expresses my soul's need—"Hear O Lord and answer" (Psalm 86:1 NIV)—or my soul's response—"Then my tongue will talk all about your righteousness; I will talk about your praise all day long" (Psalm 35:28).

> Hear me, LORD, and answer me,
>> for I am poor and needy.
> Guard my life, for I am faithful to you;
>> save your servant who trusts in you.
> You are my God; have mercy on me, Lord,
>> for I call to you all day long.
> Bring joy to your servant, Lord,
>> for I put my trust in you.
> You, Lord, are forgiving and good,
>> abounding in love to all who call to you.

Hear my prayer, Lord;
> listen to my cry for mercy.
When I am in distress I call to you,
> because you answer me.

Among the gods there is none like you, Lord;
> no deeds can compare with yours. (Psalm
86:1-8 NIV)

A woman with far more than a traditional helping of family crises and reasons for a broken heart told me she was challenged to consider what percentage of her thoughts, communication with family, social media posts, and other conversations were directly or indirectly related to her significant list of crises. When she kept track, she was appalled, and vowed to flip the statistic.

Filling her thoughts and conversations with uplifting and encouraging words converted her tune from a dirge to a much more hope-filled background accompaniment.

The soundtrack that looped through her day changed tempo and style and focus. Anyone who appreciates the power of music to shift a mood will understand what that did for her ability to cope with the difficulties she still faced.

David's musical accompaniment through the psalms soothed his soul, in some ways like the effects of the music he'd played before he became king. As a young man, he was often called upon to use his musical abilities to assuage the bouts of panic attacks or insanity—the demons—that troubled his predecessor, Saul.

Worship is the kind of soul-salve that draws poison out of a wound, the kind of antiseptic that prevents infection, and the bandage that gives the injury time to heal while focusing attention on The Healer.

Worship forms the ever-present though not always audible soundtrack that keeps our thoughts in line while God bends over us, repairing or reinforcing, bracing, holding, breathing for us.

The knitter sings out, "Hallelujah!" when the final mending stitch is secured and the garment is fully restored. The soul sings hallelujah throughout the process, worshiping even when the words are hard to form and the tune is lost.

CHAPTER EIGHT

STAINED GLASS RECOVERY

Starting Out Shattered

The beauty of stained glass is both in the image it creates, and the brokenness from which it was born.

BETHANY GREW UP IN A HOUSEHOLD THAT valued broken bits. She and her mother glued china dinner plates when they broke. "We didn't avoid setting them on the table. We used the repaired plates—cracked or shattered as they'd been—and found designs in the glue lines. I always chose the one with a design that looked like the Eiffel Tower while I dreamed of Paris," she said.

Reassembling the puzzle pieces of a broken plate became a challenge her family embraced when necessary. They felt no less sense of accomplishment than if it had been a successfully conquered jigsaw puzzle spread on the table until its picture—with lines still visible marking where one fit into another—became whole.

With a history a thousand years old, stained glass is perhaps the epitome of artistic use of bits and pieces. Stained glass by definition is glass colored from the addition of metallic salts during the manufacturing process. Metallic salts. The same elements that shatter silk can create stained glass.

Many large stained glass windows dating from the late Middle Ages remain intact today. They are held with strips of lead, like a china plate glued back together. The windows remain among the only major form of pictorial art to have survived that long. Bits. Broken or cut pieces. Shards. Limited in their beauty if alone, and too small to serve other purposes, in the hands of artists the bits shine as awe-inspiring storytellers for those observing them centuries later. Tributes to endurance. Story and strength in one work of art.

Surviving secular stained glass pieces from centuries ago are rare, we're told. Only the sacred remains.

The sacred endures.

How completely and holistically and poetically God heals us! In the Bible, physical healings were accompanied by an emotional, spiritual, or relational component...or all of the above. A son is healed and the mom gets *her* breath back. A man born blind receives his sight and, in addition, restoration to a society that now sees more clearly. A father—bereft over his son's mental illness and self-injury—watches his son freed from his demons and the *father* discovers his *own* life forever changed. No longer is his son's drama a constant source of distress. They can plan, laugh without restraint or suspicion, sleep with both eyes closed.

The mending affects far more than the person healed. And the healings reach deeper than skin and nerve endings and muscles, clear to the soul.

Like fine art, the repair's many components add an intricacy that unfolds the more they're pondered. We stand in the gallery, enamored with the artwork, pull closer for a view of brushstrokes or to see how the bits of stained glass fit together, and step back to gain the wider view. There! A detail we hadn't noticed. And there! An expression we'd missed.

Art aficionados can spend hours in front of a single painting, or days gazing at an intricate work of stained glass, extracting more and more as they focus on the artist's creation.

Our many-layered mends become part of the Master's portfolio. And evidence of our resuscitation. He is the Artful Restorer.

At a women's retreat, an attendee confessed her marriage had been in tatters less than a year earlier. Multiple stressors had shattered their vows. First she, then he responded to the Divine Invitation to "Come and heal." Her face radiant, she reported, "I didn't know our marriage could be saved, much less good!"

God made art of their mess.

Art.

Artistry has been his calling card from the beginning of creation. The most talented human artist in the world does nothing more than try to mimic or interpret the work of the Master Artist of creation.

God does nothing clumsily, awkwardly, or halfheartedly. Including healing a tattered soul. To him, it's all divine art. It's embedded in his nature. As is the compassion that moves him to tend to our woundedness.

Can you picture his response when we dump our broken pieces—a pile of sharp-edged, mismatched shards—before him? An ugly-cry surrender, an admission of our helplessness, the faint restrain of a desperate song we can barely whisper. God says, "Oh, how beautiful! Yes, yes, I can work with that!"

"Are you sure it's worth salvaging? Worth the effort?"

When asked that question, he must shake his head with incredulity. We may wonder. He doesn't. We may see a dozen reasons to give up. He sees a dozen reasons to move forward.

As if looking over a worktable strewn with bits of colored glass that once were bottles and jars, he takes delight in the art it can become—what he sees with his creative eye, not what the fractured fragments look like now.

A deep, deep soul distress related to one of my children gave me the opportunity to find out. I dumped all the pieces in front of him, hoping he could make something out of it. All I'd managed to create from the disaster was a string of sleepless nights and tear-stained pillowcases.

You may identify with why I resisted the idea of gathering with others in my faith community while no two shards of my heart connected to one another. Resistance fought against the pull toward community. I knew they'd care. I wasn't sure I could handle their concern on top of my own.

Not aware of having made a conscious decision to show up at the worship service one Sunday, I rediscovered one of the reasons gathering together with like minds and hearts is especially important for the hurting soul.

My pile of shards could—in the Artist's hands—potentially become a stained glass window. A small, decorative piece of wall art that could communicate what God can do with our shattered selves.

But when other broken people from my church added their own shards—other unique colors and shapes of pain— God could use them to create a magnificent, noteworthy, far larger and more detailed work of art.

Meeting with others who cared and who helped center me on the unchanging truths in the pages of God's word would have been reason enough. But seeing how God could make something larger if we pooled our shards into one pile of potential put me in awe.

Others have observed the same phenomenon. When we allow ourselves the benefit of community, others find voice for their hidden pain.

We loan strength to one another.

— — — — —

"This will shred me," a friend said.

How could I argue with her? Daggers of heartache sliced into her soul.

"We never anticipated triplets. It didn't cross our minds."

I held my breath for what I knew was coming next.

"We never expected to lose all three."

It didn't ease the excruciating pain to know she had other children. She'd never have the opportunity to get to know *these* three too-little ones. They died one at a time. Grief upon grief upon grief. She'd read the news story about the woman who held her stillborn baby for two hours and the child miraculously started breathing. My friend's did not. An impossible good-bye.

– – – – –

"My grandfather refused to acknowledge my mom's teen pregnancy," a friend said, explaining the distress that had kept her tattered. "My mother said he wouldn't talk about it, wouldn't talk about me, the whole time she carried me. When I was born," her voice caught in her throat for a moment, "he took me from my mom and claimed I was his daughter. The community never knew he wasn't my father. I know what that did to me. I can't imagine what it did to my mom, who her whole life had to pretend I was her little sister, not the baby who grew under her heart."

– – – – –

The middle of March in Wisconsin can be bitter cold, despite the word *spring* printed on calendars and evidence that Easter isn't far off. I don't remember the temperatures in mid-March of 2009. But I remember the funeral.

Every chair in the sanctuary held a mourner in disbelief. How could this happen? In our quiet community? A violent act cut a mother's life short as her kids stepped into adulthood. She'd talked about making better life decisions to get healthy emotionally, physically, and spiritually. About making wiser relationship choices. Her murder removed her chances of acting on those decisions.

At the end of the service, the immediate family left the sanctuary behind the pallbearers and the casket. We mourners waited for the music to start, the traditional postlude music that covers sniffles and turns peoples' thoughts toward heaven, pearly gates, flying away, meeting again someday.

The music never came.

A technical glitch in the sound system left the church completely silent except for the sound of the casket frame's wheels on the carpet. The awkwardest of silences.

The murdered woman's daughter—the youngest—held her grief in check until the procession reached the narthex. With the sanctuary doors open and no music to cover, we all heard her explosion of sobs—wracking, wrenching sobs ricocheting among the rafters. Her mother wasn't merely gone. She'd been taken. Ripped from them.

Those in the sanctuary would have tiptoed out to allow the family their private moment of intense sorrow. But we couldn't leave, couldn't move, couldn't breathe without intruding on what had become an echo chamber of abject despair for that young woman, for their whole family.

— — — — —

How does a soul heal from traumas like those?

Misery doesn't discriminate. It slaps its road sign on both affluent and poverty-stricken streets. It cozies up to people behaving themselves and those behaving badly. It doesn't seem to care whether the person has stayed long enough on misery lane or is a newcomer. It resists eviction or escape.

Sorrow creates its own poverty—an impoverishment of soul. Internal bankruptcy.

God steps boldly onto the street named Misery and sets up camp among the suffering. Like a medic, he tends the wounds and creates an environment in which even the severely tattered can mend.

Psalm 102:17 says, "God will turn to the prayer of the impoverished; / he won't despise their prayers."

The Bible relates a wrenching story of a young woman whose future was forever changed, her soul pierced and slashed, and who suffered her devastation alone, without the benefit of a faith community to hold her while she wept.

Some now reading these words will identify too deeply with Tamar's story, a story with ugliness marring every line. A story of irretrievable loss.

The Bible relates two tragic Tamar stories—two different women from different eras, both violated by men they should have been able to trust. In Genesis 38, you can read the story of Tamar, the daughter-in-law of Judah, who was married to—as one version describes him—"a particularly wretched human being" (v. 7 *The Voice*). Then life got worse. Much worse.

The other Tamar whose pain is recorded in Holy Scripture is a daughter of David, sister of Absalom and half-sister of Amnon. Her story is related in 2 Samuel 13. It's not an easy read. For some, it rings all too familiar, a twisted mirror of their own heart-wrenching distress.

Amnon had inappropriate feelings for his half-sister. He thought he loved her—man to woman—but his infatuation turned to lust, which turned to incestuous thoughts. Others were involved in the series of events that led to life's darkest moments for Tamar. Amnon's cousin Jonadab saw that Amnon was making himself sick over his feelings for Tamar. Jonadab became a just-as-sick enabler, helping concoct a scheme to lure Tamar to her brother's bedroom.

And the father who should have protected her—David— didn't. Sound familiar? He wasn't alert to the oddness of the request for David to send his virgin daughter Tamar—no one else, just her—to prepare a meal for his son Amnon, whom he adored. He asked her to "please" go.

She did. She made the meal Amnon requested. He feigned deep depression and refused to eat, sending everyone else in the room away except Tamar. He coaxed the innocent girl to bring the food closer, insisting he'd eat if she fed it to him. Then he grabbed her wrist and tried to force himself on her.

She resisted. She fought. She called what he was attempting by its real name—not love, but rape. She pleaded with him to think of both her reputation and his own. According to the culture of the day, she even suggested they could be together legally and morally if Amnon asked for her in marriage.

He overpowered her, getting what his animalistic urges demanded. Tamar was stripped of her virginity, marked with an indelible shame, her soul shattered.

Amnon's lust, which he'd mistaken for love, instantly turned to intense hate—immediately following the crime. We're told his hatred for Tamar was stronger than the love he'd previously felt for her. He tossed her out of his house.

Tamar's despair wrapped itself around her. No one could mistake that she'd been violated. She put ashes on her head and tore her long-sleeved robe—the garment virgin princesses wore. She held her head in her hands and wept. Her brother Absalom found her and took her in, but even he failed her. He convinced her to keep Amnon's sin secret. Absalom had the gall to say to her, "Don't let it bother you."

That last line capped the horror.

"So Tamar, a broken woman, lived in her brother Absalom's house" (2 Samuel 13:20).

What about her father, David? How did he respond when he found out? He got angry, but "he refused to punish his son Amnon because he loved him as his oldest child" (13:21). Not long before this incident, David had his own moral failure with Bathsheba. His story wasn't over, his spiritual mending still unfinished.

Where's the beauty, the art, in that? Those violated by incest, rape, and abuse ask that question with voices raw with their weeping. "Don't tell me God cares," they say. "Not after what I've been through."

Without minimizing the depth of their suffering and distress, it should be noted that we know about Tamar's story— you and I *know*—because God made sure her innocence would be recorded for all time in his word. Amnon, Absalom, and David tried to keep it quiet. But God knew and told the world through his servant Samuel. Tamar's tattered soul did not escape God's notice.

No tattered soul escapes God's notice.

How might the story read if Tamar had a circle of caregivers around her, heart menders who welcomed her into an atmosphere of understanding, support, healing? A church family who made who she was the focus of their attention rather than what had happened to her? People who listened, prayed, and provided a safe place for her to heal? How would the story read then?

How can any of our stories change when we reach out to God's word and his people?

"I took comfort in a single verse of Scripture," the mother who lost three babies said. "Jesus taught, 'Mourn with those who mourn.' He didn't expect me not to grieve, or to get over it quickly. He knew I would need time to keen over the loss of these children. And he gave instruction for others to join us in that soul-shattering place."

She drew a ragged breath. "Even now, these years later, I look at that one verse as a starting point on my journey to healing, both from the losses and in my connection with God. He expected I would mourn, and was okay with that. I had to be okay with it, too."

The day came when she bravely stepped back through the doors of her church, the day courage won out over isolation. Most didn't know what to say. Who would? But she stayed, because within those walls were people who cared what she and her husband had been through, what they were still going through. In that atmosphere of caring and worship, reverence for God's sovereignty and his word, and reflection on his faithfulness, her healing surged forward.

I asked her to describe the years between that horrific moment of laying her babies to rest and today. She said simply, "I was held. And so were they."

Other beautiful children. A loving and supportive husband. A faith community who rallied. Good jobs. Meaningful family life. And still, the couple couldn't escape the pulverization of this pain. No words brought mending for their excoriated souls. They found no escape hatch to free them from their circumstances. They had to walk through it, every aching day.

Every day, they slathered a fresh layer of grace ointment over the raw spots. They watched God take tiny fragments and piece them together. It was a long time before they sensed the tautness of the edges of a wound healing, hints of the picture God was creating. Even today, their wound is tender to the touch, as it should be. You can't lose something that precious and not be affected for life.

They walked their difficult journey accompanied by a faith community of people who cared, who prayed when the couple couldn't form a sentence, who served as an emotional sag wagon—like the support vehicle that accompanies bicyclists on long, grueling races—when their spirits flagged, and gentled them back into the protection of a safe place to mend.

CHAPTER NINE

ANTIQUE DOLL REDEMPTION

The Designer's Touch

*Nothing provides as fascinating a read
as the story of the wounded made whole.*

ON ONE OF THOSE SUN-BAKED FALL DAYS IN THE Northwoods when even the air is golden, four bridesmaids pulled their grape satin gowns over their heads, adjusted their updos, checked their makeup, and prepared to link arms for the procession to the starting line.

It didn't surprise onlookers that they'd chosen athletic shoes rather than heels. Or that they'd opted not to wear jewelry with their gowns. It was no surprise that music didn't signal their walk through the double doors.

Not the double doors at the back of a church sanctuary. The double doors of a barn on a farm hosting the Udder Mudder fundraising race for charity.

With five hundred other entrants, the bridesmaids slogged, crawled, climbed, and sloshed through a mud-based obstacle course for the sake of charity. They ran in the name of the young bride-to-be who lost her life in a car accident. She and her husband-to-be had been on the way home from meeting with their minister to plan the wedding ceremony. The young groom was injured, but survived, though broken in more ways than one.

Most of the bridesmaids were her sisters.

The story made national news, not only because of the tragedy, but because of the beauty of the tribute. A muddy, messed up, wild, generous tribute. Others ran the obstacle course for the rush. Or the challenge. Or for fun. Or to help out the charity. These tear-and-mud-streaked women ran to honor a vibrant life too soon gone.

They could have languished in mourning that day. Instead, they hiked up their satin gowns and tackled the course to prove that death can't get the last word. That the bride's short life meant something. And that mud can be grace-filled.

Those of us watching from the sidelines marveled at the beauty they'd wrung from a place of deep distress and loss.

Those women will never regret spending their grief that way, painting a new face on their intense pain.

— — — — —

Regrets. I've had a few.

Two of my mother's aunts attended the Chicago World's Fair. The details of their visit are buried with them. As a child, I asked too few questions about family history. That's a regret that lingers and resurfaces frequently, especially now that my mother, too, is gone.

The aunts brought two antique porcelain dolls home from the Fair and gave them to my mother. The delicate features of those dolls—eyes that opened and closed, blushed cheeks, feathered eyelashes painted on the porcelain, tiny button-top leather shoes and lace-edged pantaloons—fascinated me, although my sisters and I were not allowed to touch. The dolls sat on top of a high dresser where we could see them. That had to suffice until we were older.

Wind knocked over one of the dolls and cracked its sweet, plump-cheeked, rosebud-lipped face. Mom patched it together with whatever household glue we had on hand.

The other doll was damaged later in one of our many moves.

These details too are fuzzy, but I think I was in high school or the first year of college when my sisters and I took it upon ourselves to get the dolls repaired to surprise Mom for Christmas. We sent the dolls to a doll hospital we'd read about in a magazine. Several states away. The only one we could afford.

I sewed new pantaloons and repaired torn lace on the bodice with fabric I purchased at the local fabric store. Authenticity didn't register with me as it would today.

When the dolls were returned to us prior to Christmas that year, their faces were smooth again, but not the same. The repairer hadn't taken into consideration the type of paint originally used and hadn't consulted the antique doll guide that showed the specific coloration for that brand, style, and age of porcelain doll. The repairer had replaced the head of one of the dolls. We assumed that meant the new would match the era and style of the old. A wrong assumption.

I regret that we didn't invest in a true expert repair. I regret that we lessened the dolls' value by not investing in a proper mend.

And I regret that I failed to ask the right questions that would fill in the gaps in the story of the dolls' beginnings and a horde of other stories. You too may have wished your ancestors had kept journals or written down the family history.

I told that story to a fine art dollmaker who visibly cringed. Her eyes voiced an unspoken groan that the works of art had been mishandled by an inexpert repairer, by someone who didn't know the era, the original techniques used, and didn't value conservator-quality preservation.

An antique doll can't be repaired with any old glue, any old paint or glaze, any old fabric. It needs and deserves the attention of someone intimately acquainted with the details.

The connection to our need for our Maker and his expertise when we're broken is clear.

The dolls still have value—one lives at a sister's house now and one at mine—but the value isn't related to dollars. It's rooted in the connection—the bonding agents—with my mother and her always precocious aunts. Handled properly, the dolls could have been worth even more.

Glue. Unless it's divinely chosen glue applied the proper way, it creates more problems than answers.

When one of the large-door shelves on our refrigerator cracked along its side and bed, the split made the shelf useless. My husband—of whom I've often said, "If anyone can figure out a way to fix it, Bill can"—removed the shelf and had it patched back together with an epoxy-strength glue later that day.

He and I have been known to entertain differing viewpoints about methodology. I looked at the mend, both grateful for the speed and efficiency with which he made the repair and mystified that it hadn't occurred to him to clean the shelf first. You know those inexplicable little bits and crumbs that wind up at the bottom of a refrigerator shelf? They're now embedded in a wide, yellowish swath of epoxy, like prehistoric beetles preserved in amber.

He considered it a success because the shelf could be put back into service. Grateful for that reality, I thanked him and reinstalled the shelf. Then, a few months later, when the glue let go—because the crumbs and bits prevented a solid seal—I ordered a new shelf from the parts department.

Sometimes crumbs get trapped in the glue used in our healing. Those crumbs can weaken our soul's mend. Or we fail to consult the true Expert and attempt to repair valuable things with inferior materials. That's what usually happens when we apply a homegrown mending technique.

One of the reasons our best option for mending tattered souls is to run to the One who made us lies in the uniqueness of our injuries, pain tolerance, and emotional response.

If I told you what died, you might tell me, 'That's nothing.' And you might be right…But it was my nothing. My dream. My always. Mine. Oh, I've been through enough of these to know the drill. I'll mourn, and then, imperceptible as daylight's arrival, a little life will appear. I'll keep whining a bit, but life is relentless, and soon I'll give in to a new joy. It always happens.

Those are the insightful words from a blog post by Jonathan Friesen, friend, international speaker, and author of *Mayday* and *Both of Me*.

His confession underscores the fingerprint-like uniqueness of what tatters our souls. One person's minor detour is another's derailment. One healing journey is a steady incline from devastated to whole. Another's reads like an electrocardiograph tracing.

Nearly all would report that mending takes far longer than imagined, and more skill than expected.

"Is it really necessary, God, that we often have a long wait before we're brought to a place of wholeness, a place where we can recapture joy and stability after our soul is torn?" If you haven't asked that question, you likely know someone who has.

Is it because he gets confused over what to do for us?

He is not a God of confusion (1 Corinthians 14:33). He's fully aware—at all times—of the root of our trouble, the seismic activity in our souls, and how to mend the rifts and rips.

Is it because he takes pleasure in holding out on us? I almost apologized to God for putting those words in print, they're so ludicrous. Everything about the "holding out" concept goes against the grain of his nature. He's lavish with us. Extravagant. He's touched with our grief, the Bible tells us (Hebrews 4:15).

The artful mend shows the Almighty God bent over us like a master doll conservator or the restoration artist in the galleries of fine art, meticulously piecing together the rough edges, repairing thread by thread, matching materials and style, strengthening vulnerable areas, repainting with a brush the width of a single hair, if that's what it takes. His healing is an act of tenderness and delicateness. More neurosurgeon than fender unbender. As our Creator, he knows exactly what materials we're made of and how best to handle our soul's need.

Yet we sometimes stand over the shoulder of the restoration expert, watching fine-tipped tweezers snatch a bent thread of canvas and reposition it where it really belongs, tapping our foot and chanting, "Come on. Come on. Come on! Can't you hurry this up?"

"It's delicate work! Trust me. You don't want me to rush through this. I could, but my heart won't let me."

The restoration expert cares about the art. And about permanent repairs. And about ensuring the stability of the piece. About clearing out the crumbs and choosing the right techniques and making sure the process draws us closer to his heart. He cares about authenticity and maintaining the value through the mending. He cares about the steps along the way. He cares about the strength we gain through each step of the process.

I regret not keeping more journals through the soul mends I've experienced. It's too easy to forget the details, or to remember insignificant details and forget the important ones. When I return to journals I kept many years ago, before life grew what I thought was too busy, I can trace a pattern of growth and healing as I turn pages and read both the questions I asked God and the answers he provided. And the spaces between.

Romans 15:4 reads, "Whatever was written in the past was written for our instruction so that we could have hope through endurance and through the encouragement of the scriptures."

Will someone say that of the journals I've kept? That they found hope in the pages?

His journals are his invitation to us. Page One reads, *Come.*

"Come to me, all you who are struggling hard and carrying heavy loads, and I will give you rest" (Matthew 11:28).

Page Two: *Keep Close.*

"Come near to God, and he will come near to you" (James 4:8).

Page Three: *Keep Breathing.*

"He is the one who gives life, breath, and everything else" (Acts 17:25).

Page Four: *Keep Within My Embrace.*

"Remain in me, and I will remain in you.... If you remain in me and my words remain in you, ask for whatever you want and it will be done for you" (John 15:4, 7).

The pages of his journal urge, "Sit."

Keep Still.

"That's enough! Now know that I am God!" (Psalm 46:10).

Keep Listening.

"Let me hear what the Lord God says, / because he speaks peace to his people and to his faithful ones" (Psalm 85:8).

Keep Open.

"I pray that the eyes of your heart will have enough light to see what is the hope of God's call, what is the richness of God's glorious inheritance among believers, and what is the overwhelming greatness of God's power that is working among us" (Ephesians 1:18-19).

God whispers through his written words, "Heal."

Keep On.

"Those who stand firm during testing are blessed. They are tried and true" (James 1:12). "I press on toward the goal for the prize of the upward call of God in Christ Jesus" (Philippians 3:14 ESV).

Keep Expecting.

"Hope in the LORD! / Be strong! Let your heart take courage! / Hope in the LORD!" (Psalm 27:14). "This hope doesn't put us to shame, because the love of God has been poured out in our hearts" (Romans 5:5).

Keep Holding Out for Victory.

"But in all these things we win a sweeping victory through the one who loved us" (Romans 8:37).

Keep Following.

"So then let's also run the race that is laid out in front of us" (Hebrews 12:1).

Keep Free.

"Christ has set us free for freedom. Therefore, stand firm and don't submit to the bondage of slavery again" (Galatians 5:1).

Keep Trusting.

"Those with sound thoughts you will keep in peace, in peace because they trust in you" (Isaiah 26:3).

– – – – –

I'm beginning another journal today. I don't want to lose the details of how God responds to the places in my soul that need his touch. I hope the journal will read like a collection of psalms. Honest. Rehearsing how God answered in the past. Trusting him for the future. Confessing the times I don't understand what's happening but ending with a confident statement about the legitimate reasons to praise him while I wait.

I want my children and grandchildren to discover my journals and read the truth about a God who heals the brokenhearted and binds up their wounds, who is generous with his outrageous peace. I long for them to pour over accounts of the God who takes shards and rags and turns them into art, the God who stitches us back together with such precision that the mend is a thing of beauty.

I want them to know—both from the life I live in front of

them and the words scratched in my journal—that I draw comfort from where God's story and mine intersect. That something in me healed over when I read about a God who could make diseased, leprous skin smooth as a baby's, who could give sight to those who'd never known what it was like, who could make a mottled heart white as snow.

I long for those who come behind me to see that tattered doesn't have to be permanent.

Some entries will read, "This is hard. So hard. But God is near. So near."

Some will remain blank. Silent prayer and speechlessness look a lot alike on paper.

Some entries will read like a rant, others like a worship song.

I'll write about the way I gained empathy from what I endured. That pain sometimes brought opportunity, caution, innovation, artful redirection.

I'll use the journal to record the stories I heard when I listened to tattered souls... and leave space to record descriptions of the artwork that emerged—the mended lives they invested to help others mend.

I'll record the regrets, but not linger over them. They're too high maintenance.

At the bottom of every page, I'll write:

All the tattered souls

as a reminder to pray for them.

For you.

And on the title page, I'll add, "He has made everything [...everything...everything] beautiful in its time" (Ecclesiastes 3:11 ESV).

CHAPTER TEN

BROKEN FURNITURE REFURBISHING

Pre-Art

Only the eye of creativity sees brokenness as pre-art.

THE FARM TABLE HAD AN UNSIGHTLY BURN STAIN in the center of its surface. No doubt the result of a cast-iron Dutch oven hot off the fire or stove and no buffer—no trivet or hot pad or folded kitchen towel between its scorching surface and the table. The owner must have created a few new words in response to that faux pas. I wonder what the owner used to cover that charred place. A place mat? A centerpiece? Did the whole surface of the table have to live under the suffocating weight of a tablecloth from that moment on?

I would have been inclined to walk past the table toward other items of interest in the secondhand store. We weren't interested in something that badly damaged. But the friend with whom I shopped fell in love. With the permanently marred table. She circled it, running her hand along the smooth pine edge, never lifting her gaze from the misshapen, charred damage at its heart.

"You're not seriously thinking of—"

"Isn't it gorgeous?" She leaned in and touched the scar with her fingertips. It looked like a log pulled from a now-dead fire.

"Even at its best, before the accident, it was nothing special—a plain old farm table," I said, tugging her toward the polished tables with less of a story.

"You can't see the art?"

What art? As I looked more intently at the table, I did begin to see something worth honoring in the table's past—years of hard work reflected even in the severe burn damage. Still, I can't say I saw *art*. My friend looked at it through an artist's eyes, through creative eyes, and saw beauty emerging from its surface.

A few weeks later, the table sported a hammered copper insert where the burn scar had been. If she cared to, she could have sold the table for ten times what she paid for it in the secondhand shop. Everyone who saw it in her dining room made her an offer. Including me.

– – – – –

Minutes before a dilapidated schoolhouse had a heart-to-heart talk with a bulldozer, my husband stepped in and rescued several sets of narrow, eight-paned, oak-and-glass doors once used as cupboard doors in the science room. Dust from years of neglect, abandonment, and evidence of midnight raids by local wildlife covered the doors. But my scavenger husband knew they had potential. The door panels lived in our basement until we discovered that potential.

I can swivel my office chair and see two of them that now form glass-front doors for a chimney cupboard in this hundred-year-old farmhouse. Several more found use as a headboard for the master bedroom.

How close those doors came to demolition! Someone thought them beyond hope, not worth salvaging. Like a dust-covered marriage. Or a decimated friendship. Or a shattered family. Not worth the effort? Take a bulldozer to it?

The fireplace mantel in our family room is made from a timber pulled from a dismantled barn. The French doors that provide demarcation between the dining room and office were salvaged from an old house that was torn down more than a decade ago.

My flow-blue turkey platter—the deep blue glaze from long-gone eras flowing with intentionally blurred edges onto the white background—is too cracked to hold a turkey. It came to me that way when my aunt trimmed down her collection of antiques. No longer useful for its original intention, the platter makes intriguing wall art in my butter yellow and cobalt office. I wonder whose hands hovered over it years ago, noting yet another crack, pondering whether it could handle another gluing or if it was time to send it to the turkey-platter graveyard. I'm glad the decision was to keep it until it became art.

Creatives see brokenness as pre-art. How differently would we approach our times of spiritual or relational or emotional brokenness if we could, too? If we saw the elegant mending pattern just ahead? The artwork we could become? The craftsmanship in progress?

Among my favorite shops to explore both locally and when traveling are those filled with evidence of an artist's creativity. A repurposed dresser. A mug-sans-handle turned into a planter. The remnants of a vintage tablecloth converted into pillows. Mittens cut from discarded sweaters. Antique canning jars turned into chandeliers. Empty frames converted into chalkboard memo stations.

Not all of us can look at a broken wooden ladder or faded umbrella or incomplete set of antique flatware and envision what it can become. The creative person has no trouble seeing it as art before it is.

A friend of mine collects old flatware and with saw, vise, pliers, rasp, drill, jump rings, crystal beads, and pearls turns the handles of the mismatched pieces of silverware into bracelets. I wear mine often and purchased several to give as gifts. The repurposing starts conversations, including one with a gift recipient who said, "That was my grandmother's silver pattern. How did you know?"

I didn't. But the Artist did.

Everything about God shows his artistic bent. Hebrews 11:3 reminds us, "By faith we understand that the universe has been created by a word from God so that the visible came into existence from the invisible."

We couldn't imagine what he could create. But he saw it fully fleshed out before he spoke the words, "Let there be light. Let's start there. With light" (see Genesis 1:3). He knew that a broken Adam and a broken Eve could give birth to a planetful of people.

He knew that splits in a rock face wouldn't deface it but serve as backdrop for a crowd-pleasing waterfall.

He saw art waiting to be born as the light he created fractures into a multitude of colors when viewed through broken glass or the remnants of a storm. He knew we'd take pictures of beaches made from pulverized rock, of mosaic floors that started as bits of clay tile, of diamonds and other gems that couldn't have been uglier in their original state, buried deep underground.

That's the artistic eye. It sees pre-art in our tatteredness. Before the crisis hits, he's planned what he'll do here, and here, and here, to allow the art to emerge from the dark, cold, damp cave of pain.

We don't see it yet. We can't envision how anything remotely soul-pleasing can rise out of what shatters us. And then, one day, we notice a flash of something promising. It isn't fully formed yet, but the beauty catches us by surprise and whispers, "Hold on. This is just the beginning."

The creative say, "Don't throw away that jacket. Let me see what I can do." It's returned with artistic elbow patches or an overlay of leather on what was a torn pocket. The creative fill a bare spot in the knee of ripped jeans with a reverse applique of cotton lace or a strip of patterned fabric that peeks through the window. The creative develop handmade embellishments from felted wool to cover holes in sweaters. The creative turn a discarded crib into a love seat and broken glass into a one-of-a-kind backsplash. Creatives thrive on discovering a place for their creativity to land.

Turning the copper inset tables on end…

When we find a creative outlet while we're healing, we can align ourselves with the Creator who mends us. My mother knit blankets even after she'd been admitted to a hospice residence facility. Some days she couldn't see or focus or hold the project as she weakened. But as long as she could, she knitted.

Many of the most poignant songs—including those from early history—were created from a place of soul ache. Writing poetry is a creative outlet that gives expression to emotions that need art to do them justice. Do you garden your way through grief? Or create fused glass beads? Do you find wound-threatening tension dissipating when you dance or paint or scrapbook or create pottery?

The art of healing the wounded soul—the subtitle of the

book in your hands—includes the art we create while mending. Stories we write. Journals we keep. Photographs we take. Music we play or compose or both. Broken things we upcycle, clinging to the parallel of what we're watching happen within us.

Within my circle of friends is a woman who holds tightly to a long-honored and nearly forgotten tradition of penmanship as an art form. I watch as she turns to a fresh page in her notebook, uncaps her fountain pen, and writes as if allowing her pen a slow waltz. One letter. Two. Connected. Scrolling. As I watch, my blood pressure drops, so soothing is the motion of her pen on paper. She's an active, successful businesswoman. I wonder if artistic penmanship is one of her creative outlets in a world that eats *hurry* for breakfast.

And I wonder how much easier it would be for me to heal from soul traumas if I slowed the speed of my pen. And my texting thumbs. I wonder if some of the creative outlets I once enjoyed would help revive my soul, not just revitalize an art form.

Part of the invitation to mend when so many around us are resigned to leaving things tattered is God calling us into a creative process with him. He mends artistically and invites us to create with him. *With* the Creator.

Every broken thing we make beautiful is an investment in our healing. Every soul we soothe reflects back to soothe the tatters we bear. Every culinary gift we share with others feeds something within us. Every time we attempt to capture the nuances of nature in an image, sculpture, or painting, we're celebrating what God can do, and bracing or fortifying our faith in his ability to sketch beauty across the fabric of our souls.

> God created humanity in God's own image,
> in the divine image God created them,
> male and female God created
> them. (Genesis 1:27)

In the divine creative image, he created us. It's no surprise, then, that he takes delight in finding us engaged in the creative process. The aware artist senses him near when blowing glass, designing a brochure or a building, pulling a pastry from the oven, making paper, stringing beads, setting a precious stone in silver.

The act of creation draws him near, or draws us near to him. There's healing in his presence. No wonder so many wounded find the hope they longed for during the process of creating, singing, worshiping, painting. Hope hangs thick where he is present.

Have you watched what happens in a hospital room?

Caring creatives, aching from the news of the heart attack that flattened the one they love, arrange flowers and cards to make them more aesthetically pleasing. Then, they re-arrange. And might the next day, too. Instinctively, they create even in the midst of distress.

We hear stories of bands in Third World countries using instruments created from cereal boxes and gas cans, make-shift choirs who sang through wars, the eight-piece orchestra whose music played "Nearer, My God, to Thee" as the *Titanic* sank. Journalist Steve Turner drew insights about the power of creativity in the midst of crisis from John Carr, one-time coworker of the Titanic's orchestra leader Wallace Hartley. "I know he [Hartley] often said that music was a bigger weapon for stopping disorder than anything on earth. He knew the value of the weapon he had, and I think he proved his point."

Creativity itself—art—in the wounded seasons, changes things. If not outcomes, it changes us internally.

Nail art for a bedridden daughter.

A memory album for a dementia patient and family.

A meal for a hurting family, plated on fine china, with cloth napkins, and a gourmet dessert. Just because.

In some prisons, art programs steer the incarcerated to-ward creative pursuits. The end result is a portfolio of paintings and a matching portfolio of life-change. Inner-city youth programs find temperaments of at-risk youth redirected when they connect to an artistic or musical outlet for their anger, hostility, fear, despair.

From God's perspective—the ultimate Creative—brokenness is pre-art.

How does that temper our experience when we've been hollowed by betrayal or loss, sliced open by injustice, worn to a thread by caregiving or medical treatments or estrangement or slander? How can it matter that God sees art when we still see only an open, raw wound?

The ugliness we're experiencing—you and I—is a precursor to God-autographed artwork ahead. Fortified by that fact, we hold on for the mending. We resist the thought that *tattered* is the new *healthy*, and instead lean into the process that ends in art.

God remolded a shepherd boy into a king. He created a lineage for Jesus from a harlot. He shaped Moses into a leader and transformed a borrowed tomb into the scene of a world-rocking moment made famous by its emptiness. He restored families and fortunes, elevated servants, and used his creativity to silence the haughty. He took a ball of clay and formed a human, hovered over the chaos, and offered it hope.

That God. That's the one. The one who hovers over you and me with a heart of compassion itching to make art out of our messes, to stitch together our gaping wounds and present us to the world as evidence of his artistry.

Faith tells us God sees the art that isn't yet born in us.

"God has prepared things for those who love him that no eye has seen, or ear has heard, or that haven't crossed the mind of any human being" (1 Corinthians 2:9).

I think I'll uncap a fountain pen and carve that promise in slow-forming, waltz-like letters as a reminder that he sees what I can't—what it's becoming.

CHAPTER ELEVEN

JEWELRY REGENERATION

Unfixable but Mendable

God has the heart of an artist. He can't help it.
Everything he touches becomes art.

WHEN I SPEAK ON THE SUBJECT OF MENDING THE
tattered soul, I often wear a distinct piece of jewelry—a statement necklace I purchased at a boutique that specializes in
upcycled items destined for the scrap heap, wastebasket, or
landfill. Throw pillows made from worn chenille bedspreads.
A tattered piece of sheet music reborn as the covering for a
keepsake container. Bookshelves and flower boxes from converted bicycle baskets.

And the necklace.

It caught my eye every time I visited the store. Displayed against the backdrop of a simple black sheath dress, it hung lightly as if draped around the neck of an invisible but appreciative woman. A conversation-starter necklace, with a series of graduated shield-like flat panels completely covered with vintage earrings, brooches, decorative pins. Bits without their backs or chains or mates remade into an elegant statement piece that had no trouble communicating.

After my fourth or fifth trip to the store, it surprised me to see the necklace still there. Waiting. Waiting for me to realize it clearly illustrated the principle that God's soul-repair work is not just good but poetic, artistic. I finally got the message. The necklace begged to accompany me to speaking engagements. It wasn't costly. But it voiced a memorable and potentially life-changing principle.

God is a Master in the art of refurbishing. Layering. Elegant patching. French seams that tuck ragged edges under so they can't unravel further. Creative hemming. Replacing worn collars. Embellishing cuffs. Adding an applique, a button, artful jewelry to what we assume a lost cause. He knits us together in our mother's womb, Psalm 139:13 tells us, and reknits us when we unravel.

"Come-sit-heal" is an invitation to his easel, to his potter's wheel, his embrace, his intensive care unit, his jewelry counter and stained glass studio, his restoration chamber, his retreat. It's an invitation to move beyond tattered to where the mended places form traceable yet tender tracks of where his love has been.

A woman in our neighborhood called to share a soul-crushing story with a tender stitch of healing in it. "Isn't it the worst pain when your kids are hurting?" she started. "I tried to do the dishes, the laundry, anything to keep busy and not stop long enough to think about what was happening. When I finally crashed, the tears came. I looked at my husband and said, "I just feel so scattered!" He held out his arms and said, "Come here. I'll help collect you."

Like a bin of discarded jewelry orphans transformed to a statement piece.

Among my treasured possessions is an antique pocket watch that once belonged to a great-uncle on my mother's side, passed on to me through my grandfather. The gold-plated engraved cover pops open with a push on the stem to reveal a watch face that saw perhaps a hundred years of service before it stopped working. Over time, the watch hands fell off and have been lost.

I could purchase replacement hands, but that wouldn't

make the watch function again. It is broken at a soul level. Deep inside. Its inner workings are cracked, rusted, or missing essential pieces.

The filigree engraving on the case is intricate, no doubt handcrafted by a master watchmaker or jeweler, an artisan. Even with its lid closed, it's a beautiful work of art. It's not functioning now for what it was designed. I can appreciate it in its inert state. But it was created for so much more.

As are we.

We can keep our shell or case polished and in shape—harder for some of us than others—but there's more to our value than that. What were we created for? And who do we belong to?

I wear the watch on a chain around my neck as a piece of jewelry. But there's no point in pressing the stem anymore to look at those ancient black hands against the off-white face, tracing a circle past the hedge of Roman numerals. The hands are gone. The spring inside, silent.

Some of us think that's all we can expect. A friendship died. So be it. We've grown inert in our once-vibrant faith. It was for a season. A marriage crumbles, and we see it as part of our history, not as something we should invest in, find the expert, do the homework, pay the price so it can be restored.

People are tattered. Some say, "Then let's make tattered fashionable." But God invites us to mend.

Healthy souls have stronger fibers. They can bear more of the world's sharp edges without tearing. And if torn, they can mend. That means one thing when the "inciting incident"— as novelists call it—is past. The injuries from the car accident are healed. Another perhaps better job is yours, making you just shy of grateful for your previous company's downsizing. The years of infertility have ended. You or someone you care about has been crowned Cancer Free.

The cry, "I want to see" asks for insights into what good came from the lean years or the excruciating distress. How did it make you stronger? Who is helped by having seen you come out on the other side?

It's another plea entirely when a person is still in the middle of unfinished pain.

The tour of duty is completed. Honorable discharge. But the nightmares and panic attacks won't stop. The abuse ended years ago. The too-vivid memories color every waking and sleeping moment. The child born with severe disabilities is now twenty-three and still can't hold his head up or speak your name. The son who flirted with trouble in high school is paying for the trouble he found. Another twelve years behind bars.

Or the distress has no endpoint.

You know her (or him). She's made an occupation out of her pain. It's all she talks about. It consumes her, waking and sleeping. When she can sleep. No matter the conversation, it will find its way to her unmendable circumstances, the tatters of her soul. She (or he) is exceptionally gifted at finding a way to turn everything into a negative, turn trauma into drama.

But no one could blame her for mourning the wreckage, the devastation in her life. What happened to her those years ago at the hand of that teacher/uncle/employer/unfaithful spouse/church leader/abusive parent/rapist/terrorist/so-called friend defines the words *inexpressible* and *reprehensible*. Soul-shattering.

If you are that person, please know the list was not meant to lump your pain with others' or minimize the horror done to you and the scraping of your soul, to categorize it with a cadre of other hurts as if yours is not unique and uniquely trying. What the list does, tragically, is show—once again—that you are not alone.

Friends watch for a small crumb of hope. "Good day at work today." Or "Isn't that a gorgeous sunset?" They anticipate the ever-present tagline, "But I probably won't sleep tonight. I never do. Not without nightmares."

The tattered soul is consumed by the pain, by the need to relive, rehearse, and rehash how horrible it was... but at what price?

Pain is not a choice. Obsession with our pain is, in its seedling stages. When we allow it to grow out of control, it overshadows everything—even what we once held as important, essential, or precious to us—and becomes more addiction than choice.

We don't choose our pain. But follow-up choices when we're broken will lead us toward healing or lock us in perpetual brokenness.

A family in a community near me talks soberly about the attention they felt compelled to show their severely disabled son. Little else happened—within the walls of their home or outside of it—that didn't relate somehow to the boy's needs. What devotion! But the day dawned when they realized that subconsciously the child had become their obsession rather than their son—a series of tasks rather than the product and object of their love.

This family's resolution came in an admirable way that tugs at the hearts of those who know them. They invited two disabled foster boys—siblings—into their home. The boys had fewer physically demanding needs than their son, so the family they created gave their son brothers, gave a loving home to the foster children, and helped these parents return to a healthier outlook. Laughter returned. The concept of *family* replaced obsession.

Their story is uniquely theirs. And exquisitely beautiful. What had kept them bound became a catalyst to loving larger, serving farther, and finding within that outreach the stirrings of heart healing. And a burgeoning supply of gratitude.

Not all obsessions end in artwork. Some spiral ever downward to a shadowy place labeled "Unmendable."

I've seen too many *befores* and *afters* to give up hope. People I thought were broken beyond repair, or had made choices that sealed their destinies in a tomb or cell, now walk free. I've seen the least-likelies and the not-a-chances become the leaders and the waymakers. I've served under and beside those who were given negative percentages for living through what they experienced. And I read about a wealth of them every time I open my Bible.

But I've also seen the face of evil in a conscience-devoid abuser, looked into the emptiness of drug-doped eyes, felt the air chill in the presence of a chronic deceiver or pathological liar, tasted the bitterness of someone else's hatred. I've listened to the emotionally maimed struggle to draw a breath. Wrapped my arm around the shoulders of the perpetually despairing. And seen the fallout of sin's domino effect on a family.

Thomas the Doubting One thought his faith torn beyond repair. Known for his pessimism and skepticism, he earned his nickname honestly. Then he heard unbelievable news. His friend Jesus, alive again? Impossible. Hope had been ripped to bloodied shreds on a cruel cross. But the story turned out to be true. Death? Defeated. Hopelessness? Trounced.

The Doubter's soul was mended so thoroughly that it's said Thomas may have traveled farther to tell others about Jesus than any of the other apostles. His work in India is legendary. He may have gone as far as China with his hope-giving message.

What a transformation!

Unfixable and unmendable are two different entities. A loved one dead and buried is gone. In this life, that won't be reversed. A childhood stolen by evil can't be relived. Physical and emotional consequences of a lifetime of bad decisions aren't always fixable.

But a tattered soul can be mended.

A woman pulled her car to the drive-thru window of a

local coffee shop. The caffeinated employee at the window asked, "And how can I make this an outstanding day for you today?" His version of, "What'll you have, lady?"

She smiled, thanked him for her coffee and his cheerful customer service and later told me, "What if I'd expressed what was really on my heart? 'How can you make it an outstanding day? Can you arrange to have my husband released from prison?'"

Some things can't be fixed. But they can be mended.

Like that woman's marriage. Though tattered by her husband's criminal activity, their marriage started the rebuilding process shortly after his arrest, long before his sentencing. They determined not to become a prison statistic, and that, despite his legitimate need to pay his debt to society, they would find a way to emerge from his imprisonment with their marriage stronger than ever.

It began with his brokenness. They both knew it had to start there. Pride fell away in great, tear-drenched chunks. He humbled himself before his wife, his family, and his God. It had to start there.

Then the two of them conducted an assessment of what they knew to be true. With the "house" gutted, what was left? The foundation and bare walls. Enough to rebuild. Their foundation had been driven deep into bedrock. God had brought them together, knowing full well what was ahead. God heals broken things. God can do the impossible. Marriage is worth the effort.

They couldn't erase what led to the crisis, but they could both make decisions from that moment on—a new twist on their vows' "from this day forward."

It's a recurring theme for people who find themselves in trouble:

Mending a tattered soul is unrelated to the inability to change the past.

— — — — —

A new friend shared her can't-change-the-past story. "When my mother was nine years old—an only child—my grandmother told her, 'Had I known what caused babies, you'd not have been born.'"

Imagine trying to navigate preadolescence, the teen years, and into adulthood with that blistering legacy. Imagine the searing loneliness, the devastation to a fragile soul!

"My mother was criticized for every move she made," my friend said. "She vowed no child she knew would ever experience the hollowness she'd known, that she would cherish however many children God would give her when she married. We *were* cherished," she said. "All seven of us. My dad was devoted to my mom and was a tremendous role model for the four of us daughters when it came to finding heroes of our own. He was an exceptional role model for my three brothers in how to treat a woman. My mother chose well, both in the man she married and in her determination not to repeat the hurt she'd been caused. She used the injury to her soul as a springboard to create a new legacy. With God's nurturing and his grace propelling her, she helped establish a heritage of cherishing children who grew up to cherish children."

Art. From broken shards.

My friend's mother couldn't point to an idyllic childhood. History didn't change. Her mending came despite her history. It was born in the depths of her soul as a God-fueled determination to love right, despite the childhood she'd been handed. She healed as she loved.

Fixed isn't always the goal. Stronger. Yes, stronger. That's a good goal.

"You may not control all the events that happen to you," wrote the late author, poet, and life-observer Maya Angelou, "but you can decide not to be reduced by them."

Decide? Some would argue it's not as easy as deciding. Some would throw this book against the wall—or just did—at the absurdity that making a decision has anything to do with mending.

We can't erase memories. We can't flip a switch and not be troubled by the past. We can't choose a date on the calendar as our personal Get Over It Day. Or mend by wishing hard enough until it appears.

We can't change the events of the past or ignore their repercussions. But we can reframe them in context.

Some approach memories as if they carry a power beyond serving as piercing reminders of our hurt. Those injured souls see memories as *legitimizers* of their hurt. So despite the ugliness, the sting, the damage unframed memories cause, they're invited to sink their roots into the fabric of life.

The hurting who respond to the Divine Invitation to reframe their flashbacks and nightmares and too-vivid memories can pave the way for a deeper and surer soul healing.

It changes little but our approach. But changing our approach and the way we view what happened to us can change our soul status from unmendable to mending to mended.

I spoke with a woman whose grown children have not only broken her heart with their addictions and self-destructive choices, but are working hard to discredit her. Publicly. They seem bent on making her suffer for unknown sins, as if belittling her could take the spotlight off their personal miseries. If they refuse to let her see her grandchildren, that will serve her right, won't it? If they air their grievances with their mom over the Internet, they'll cut more deeply, won't they? More than one mom in history has felt unappreciated. This mom is vilified in that sometimes-helpful-sometimes-destructive forum of social media.

Her mangled heart struggles to keep pumping, despite the smear campaign coordinated by the children to whom she gave birth and raised through their father's alcoholism and wandering eyes.

She admits that at times anger threatens to overwhelm her. But those seeking her emotional harm win another battle if she allows that to happen. So she holds on, ignores what she can, prays for her children to find peace and freedom, and redirects her energies to activities that promote her own healing while she's waiting for theirs to kick in.

It's a family shredded so thoroughly, reason would tell us there's no point in hoping for restoration. Too much resentment among them. Too many years of relentless backstabbing. Too much territory lost to the war.

Who could accurately predict the outcome? The God to whom she's turning is limitless in power, and equally limitless in compassion. We know he hears the prayers of the brokenhearted. We also know from experience, from what we read in passages throughout the Bible, and in specific sections like Hebrews 11, that some reach life's end without seeing the fulfillment of their prayers.

How will her story end? She doesn't know. The rift between her and her children seems unmendable. And it may be. But her actions are the only sensible—and only God-honoring—actions she could take, not knowing the long-term outcome.

If she keeps her anger in check and moves bravely forward, grateful for the smallest victory—continuing to love the hard-to-love, even if her children's hearts never turn back to her—she will have won a personal victory. Still heartbreaking? Certainly. Nowhere near her ideal or the outcome she longs for. But she will have preserved an atmosphere in which God can heal her soul despite the offenses against it.

Ask those who maintain their grip on joy despite chronic pain. Unmendable? Their condition may be unmendable, this side of heaven. But their soul can be a canvas for God's artful restoration. And gratitude provides the frame.

I follow several bloggers who provide an online community for the chronically ill. One is pointedly devoted to those whose illnesses don't show on the outside. Theirs may be the toughest journeys. They share common ground with those whose wounds are emotional—unseen but no less real than visible distresses of an amputee or anorexic, a burn victim, a bald and browless cancer patient.

Our hearts soar when we see an amputee not only adjusting to his artificial limb but running marathons. We don't even *know* to soar when the chronically but invisibly ill make it through their son's softball game despite the fiery pain singeing their nerve endings.

We applaud when the cancer patient whips off her wig to show a half-inch of hair growth...and a bright smile. A gladiator wins a heroic battle, claiming her life is somehow richer because of having conquered cancer, more alert to the ordinary joys. We don't see or hear about the victory when the veteran with PTSD manages to join the family for fireworks at the Fourth of July celebration.

"This is who I am now," a woman said, explaining the personality alterations and cognitive struggles brought on by brain injury she suffered in a near-fatal collision. "I'm not the same. I know it. Everyone else knows it. But strangers don't, because the—the"—she fought for the word—"changes don't show on the outside. I look as normal as I ever did."

I could hear it in her voice. In the hesitations and word searches. A young woman who'd been a spitfire teacher. Teaching had been taken off the table by the accident and its fallout. Slowly, she'd worked her way to a place of productivity and hope, grappling for every inch of progress. But she might forever fight the battle to be understood.

Her young children try, but find the erratic mood swings uncomfortable. So does she. Her husband—God love him—stays by her side through it all, despite how different she is from her earlier self, from the woman to whom he'd pledged his forever.

She's still making progress. The short-range view makes her brain injury seem unmendable, as if how far she's come is all she can hope for. She's determined to keep working on the physical and occupational therapy exercises, and to continue the counseling that helps her understand what's happened to her and how to adjust around what's gone, irreparably damaged, or slow to heal. On her best days, she's consumed by gratitude that her life was spared.

The initial prognosis is such a contrast to where she is now that she's known around her town as a walking miracle. But barring another miracle, some of what she and her family bear will be part of the fabric of their lives from this point on.

Mending for her—as for many of us—is many layered. Mind. Body. Soul.

The medical and psychological communities are working on her mind and body mends. Her connection and attention to the Lover of her soul is impacting the other vital layer of her healing. To the One who loves her soul. To the Artist who does a better job of mending ragged places than we could imagine.

She's reframing her distress, taking an accurate view of the pain that is past versus what still lingers with hope for where she'll be a few years from now.

Gratitude frames the canvas for the healing work yet to come.

A dark-eyed toddler daughter of friends is rewriting the book of manners. She doesn't stick out her small hand, palm up, and say, "Please?" when she wants something. "Please, may I have a pickle?"

Instead, those bright eyes light up as she extends her hand and says, "Thanks, pickle." She's already in the thanking stage before she ever asks.

Adults around her find it adorable. And life-altering.

What would happen if we approached our God that way? With gratitude the first words out of our mouths and expectation that he will provide? "Thanks, mending. Thanks, endurance. Thanks, peace. Amen."

– – – – –

I can't know what brought you to this book. I know what brought me. The tattered whom I love and the tattered that I've sometimes been.

An artist showed me how she creates braided scarves from vintage fabrics. She starts by ripping the fabric into strips before she weaves them together. "The best end products come from the pre-tattered," she said, unaware how deeply those words would resound with someone writing a book about tattered souls, and about the Divine Invitation to "Come and mend."

This is a book of ongoing invitation. It isn't "splash a bucket of paint on the canvas" art, but meticulous, careful, intricate work done on that most fragile and delicate of spaces—the human soul. Art from the heart of the Master—the Creator and Lover of our souls.

A two-word phrase reverberates between the lines on these pages—*Only God.*

Can I find mending for my bruised places? For my threadbare faith? For my shattered relationships and shards of myself? For my lifetime of never enoughs and not agains?

If those are the questions you're asking, or the questions you hear the people you care about asking, the answer is yes, with a qualifier.

Only God.

Linger over these heartening verses. Skimming will give you an idea. Lingering will give hope:

> *Only in God* do I find rest;
>> my salvation comes from him.
> *Only God* is my rock and my salvation—
>> my stronghold!—I won't be shaken any-
>>> more....
> Oh, I must find rest in *God only*,
>> because my hope comes from him!
> *Only God* is my rock and my salvation—
>> my stronghold!—I will not be shaken.
> My deliverance and glory *depend on God.*
>> *God* is my strong rock.
>> My refuge is *in God.*
> All you people: Trust in him at all times!
>> Pour out your hearts before him!
>> *God is our refuge!* (Psalm 62:1-2, 5-8,
>>> *emphasis mine*)

Faith in the God who inspired that confidence doesn't make healing easy. It makes it possible.

"He will create calm with his love; / he will rejoice over you with singing" (Zephaniah 3:17). Like a tapestry artist who sits back to admire his work, lays aside his needle, and takes delight in the mended you he sees.

BEYOND THE END

As You Mend

1. Take a deep breath. Some of this will sting.

2. Intentionally relax resistance muscles. Allow God to do what he longs to do for and in you.

3. Do what you can to create an atmosphere for mending. Set boundaries that allow you to heal. You need every advantage. That might mean saying no to stress producers until the healing has "caught."

4. Admit regrets, but rehearse hope. Give up fruitless blame fixing. Searching for the person to blame occupies time and energy needed for healing. It keeps us from cleaning up the spilled milk before it destroys the hardwood floor.

5. From among the hundreds of possibilities, select several key Scripture verses to serve as focal points while you mend.

6. Refuse to entertain untrue thoughts about yourself, your past, your worth in God's eyes, and the healing on its way.

7. Be patient with yourself and with the undulations of the process—rapid progress then slower-paced, weeks of victory and a day of setback before break-through again. As the adage reminds us, giving up on something this important because of a setback is like slashing the other three tires because one is flat.

8. Reassure yourself frequently that, despite how it sometimes feels, God's attention is fully trained on you (Psalm 139:17-18).

9. Don't fake joy. But don't turn down its offer.

10. Hold onto the mend as it comes. Abandon yourself to the artfulness of healing.

MENDING PRAYERS

- It never pays to be dishonest with God. If you need to, tell him, "God, I'm not seeing the art in this. All I see is shattered threads." He's heard it before. He'd rather have your honesty than your platitudes.

- If you pray, "God, it hurts," he hears that cry and answers, "I know." When the healing hasn't yet come, his understanding can serve as a life raft of hope.

- "Father God, make me braver than I feel."

- Courageously pray, "God, please override the crippling feeling that this will ruin me forever. I want to believe your truth about me and about you. It's not coming naturally."

- Some feel worthless, broken, frayed out of habit. Don't let that be you. In your times of prayer, ask God to convince you how he feels about you.

- "God, my True Father, with your help, I'll finish stronger than I am today. Wiser. An overcomer and a champion of peace."

- Pray one of the psalms back to God. Start with a chapter like Psalm 56. It contains verses like this one that reassure you of God's level of interest in what you're going through. "You yourself [God] have kept track of my misery. / Put my tears into your bottle— / aren't they on your scroll already?" (Psalm 56:8).

- "God, you know me better than I know myself. I give you permission to reveal anything I'm doing that hinders or unnecessarily prolongs this healing process. I'm listening."

- Philippians 4:6 invites us to spill all our "prayers and petitions." "In every circumstance and in everything, by prayer and petition (definite requests), with thanksgiving, continue to make your wants known to God" (AMP). If you wonder if the prayer on your heart qualifies, be assured it does. Even if it is no more spiritual sounding than, "God, I need to know this matters to you."

- Note that the following verse, Philippians 4:7, says that when we tell him our needs and thank him for the answers, "*then* the peace of God that exceeds all understanding will keep [our] hearts and minds safe in Christ Jesus" (emphasis mine). Peace. Mending. They share a lot in common.

- Consider using the lyrics of a hymn or worship song as your prayer.

- "I'm yours, Lord. I spread my brokenness out before you, trusting you to make something out of it, something we both can live with."

- "God of Immeasurable Patience, you know I've tried a thousand things to find relief for the ache in my soul. I've heard your Divine Invitation. Here I am."

STRETCHING TO MEND

- Find an object that reminds you God can make art from broken pieces—a mosaic tile, a small bit of stained glass, a refurbished lamp, a purchase from a secondhand store. Or, perhaps, just begin to see differently the chipped plate you never use but haven't been able to throw away. Keep it near you as a visible reminder of the Divine Invitation to mend.

- Find a place where the air is clear and fresh. A park. A lake. Your garden. A woodland path. Spend at least a few minutes there focused on nothing but breathing more deeply than has become your habit. Steady, slow, deeper breathing. And listening. God's comfort resides in the silent moments. Reset the pace of your concern that way.

- Is there something around the house that needs a repair you've put off too long? A doorknob that needs tightening. A hinge that hangs loose. A shirt missing a button. A small spot on the wall that needs a paint touch-up. Time yourself as you complete that project today. How long did it take? How long did you procrastinate? What's that math look like? Use the exercise as a reminder that mending is possible even for the long-broken.

- Commit to memory a few key verses, or even one, that will help sustain you during the most difficult moments of mending. Pull them out when you need them. Verses like: "Whenever I'm afraid, / I put my trust in you— / in God, whose word I praise. / I trust in God; I won't be afraid. / What can mere flesh do to me?" (Psalm 56:3-4). Or divide this passage into three or four parts, rehearsing them until they're ingrained in the fabric of your tattered soul.

- Watch a video of art restoration. Note the similarities in the tenderness and meticulousness of the art restorer and God's careful mend.

- Choose one thing each day to intentionally remove the perception that the shatters in your soul are lapping over into your relationships with your family and friends. Read a story to your children. Stick a love note on your spouse's steering wheel. Write an encouraging post to a friend...with no mention of your soul's crisis. Yes, you're too exhausted to give. Try the small, five-minute gestures. As your other relationships grow stronger, your healing has a better chance.

- Create a screen saver or computer/phone wallpaper from a favorite photograph and include the words: Prayer + Gratitude = Peace.

- Cue a worship song or hymn so it's the first thing you hear in the morning, as you make breakfast, brush your teeth, shower. Let it serve as a backdrop for another day of trusting as you mend.

- When life's flowerbed is a tangle of weeds, zoom in for the close-up. The faces of your children. The safe home in which you now sit compared to the dangerous one from which you escaped. The sun chasing shadows. Dew—what a magnificent invention. Spend more and more time in the other, unscarred places of life.

- Reserve a half hour with you, God, and a pen and notebook. Write down what you believe is unmendable. On the facing page, reframe that thought in context, even if you don't see or feel its truth yet.

- The soul is a sluggish mender when the body is mistreated. We can't expect the seat of our emotions to mend if we're not sleeping, not eating, breathing air stagnated by bitterness and regret. God understands even that. Psalm 102:4 reads, "My heart is smashed like dried-up grass. / I even forget to eat my food / because of my intense groans." Don't wait until you feel like eating or feel like forgiving. Now is good.

- What did you once love to do that has become distasteful to you, or seems to require too much energy in this Valley of Achor? Do that. For a few minutes. Then try it again tomorrow for another few minutes. Then mark space for it on your calendar. Live while you're healing.

WITH DEEPEST
GRATITUDE

Moving a mending concept from theory to hope is a combination of two key factors—the God who promises, and the people who have stories to tell about the art He makes from their messes. My gratitude runs oceans deep to both.

I'm grateful, too, for artisans through the centuries and in our neighborhoods who demonstrate the breath-stealing results when the broken, ragged, or ordinary are transformed into the noteworthy.

The people whose stories form the connections in this book that is in itself an example of broken pieces rearranged, reformed, restored, redefined, have chosen to remain anonymous. In some cases, their mending is still in process.

I'm deeply grateful for the editors whose fingerprints have

left impressions on the pages—Lil Copan, Lauren Winner, Ramona Richards, Katie Johnston; and to Cat Hoort, Brenda Smotherman, Sonua Bohannon, Susan Salley, and so many others at Abingdon Press who invest themselves in seeing books move from idea to pages to the hands of readers.

Unending gratitude to my agent, Wendy Lawton, from Books & Such Literary Management, whose wisdom and compassion compete to outdistance each other.

Brilliant light shines through the stained-glass window formed by those who committed to pray for me as I wrote, including close friends, family members, fellow writers, and the faith community I call home.

Knowing my husband prayed me through this manuscript, and every book I write, is a treasure I hold close to my heart. Thank you, Bill, for the way you're adjusting your life around what God is doing in both of us.

NOTES

2. Sashiko and Boro Rescue

"Forgiveness doesn't excuse (other people's) behavior."

Interview with authors Justin and Trisha Davis about their book *Beyond Ordinary: When a Good Marriage Just Isn't Good Enough* (Carol Stream, IL: Tyndale House, 2012) in Trisha Davis, "Beyond Ordinary Forgiveness," incourage (blog), April 10, 2013, http://www.incourage.me/2013/04/beyond-ordinary-forgiveness.html.

3. Quilt Reconstruction

Vintage clothing experts tell us shattered

Nicole Jenkins, "Vintage 101—Shattering Silk," Circa Vintage (blog), June 5, 2013, http://circavintageclothing.com.au/2013/06/05/shattering-silk/.

4. Metal Recycling

Yes, art communities. A few green patina tiles

Jeff Lea, "New Exhibition at Lambert Airport Explores Many Forms of Art," Lambert St. Louis International Airport (blog), December 3, 2014, http://flystl.com/Newsroom/Blog/tabid/422/categoryid/7/Default.aspx.

"There's a battle to be waged"

Andrew Wagner, "The Metropolitan Struggles to Keep Opera Alive," Artfcity (blog), July 21, 2014, http://artfcity.com/2014/07/21/the-met ropolitan-struggles-to-keep-opera-alive/.

6. Fine Art Reclamation

"Of course, you grow attached"

"The Process of Art Restoration" video of the Buffalo State College Art Conservation Department, September 6, 2011, https://www.youtube.com/watch?v=Nal8zLsPXwg.

"vitality in all of its breadth"

Trent C. Butler, ed., entry for "Soul," Holman Bible Dictionary, http://www.studylight.org/dictionaries/hbd/view.cgi?n=5974. 1991.

10. Broken Furniture Refurbishing

"I know he [Hartley] often said that music"

Steve Turner, "What Did the Titanic Band Play On?" FoxNews.com, April 9, 2012, http://www.foxnews.com/opinion/2012/04/09/why -did-titanic-band-play-on/.

11. Jewelry Regeneration

"You may not control all the events that happen to you"

Excerpted from Maya Angelou, *Letter to My Daughter* (New York: Random House, 2008).

Also Available from Award-Winning Author Cynthia Ruchti

"OFFERS HOPE THAT GOD CAN DO A MIGHTY WORK EVEN WITH THOSE OF US WHO CARRY THE UGLIEST OF SCABS."

—DEBBIE MACOMBER, #1 *New York Times* bestselling author

SURVIVING THE FALLOUT of
OTHER PEOPLE'S CHOICES

Ragged Hope

CYNTHIA RUCHTI

**Ragged Hope: Surviving the Fallout
of Other People's Choices**
Paperback: 9781426751172 | $15.99
Ebook: 9781426770814 | $15.99

Stories Hemmed in Hope
From Award-Winning Author and Speaker Cynthia Ruchti

They Almost Always Come Home
Paperback: 9781426702389 | $14.99
Ebook: 9781426715433 | $14.99
Hardcover: 9781630888145 | $24.99

When the Morning Glory Blooms
Paperback: 9781426735431 | $14.99
Ebook: 9781426770777 | $14.99
Hardcover: 9781630888107 | $24.99

All My Belongings
Paperback: 9781426749728 | $14.99
Ebook: 9781426787324 | $14.99
Hardcover: 9781630888152 | $24.99

As Waters Gone By
Paperback: 9781426787270 | $14.99
Ebook: 9781630887919 | $14.99
Hardcover: 9781630889302 | $24.99

www.AbingdonFiction.com

I can't unravel, I'm

HEMMED

in *hope*

For more information on speaker and author Cynthia Ruchti:

🅕 Cynthia Ruchti Reader Page   🐦 @CynthiaRuchti   CynthiaRuchti.com

CPSIA information can be obtained at www.ICGtesting.com
Printed in the USA
BVOW05*1304170715

409030BV00002B/3/P